LIFE OF THE INCAS
IN ANCIENT PERU

LIFE OF THE INCAS
IN ANCIENT PERU

Text by
Jésus and Lucienne Romé

Translated by Peter J. Tallon

Liber

Contents

© Editions Minerva, S. A. Genève, 1978
Printer, industria gráfica sa
Tuset, 19 Barcelona Sant Vicenç dels Horts 1978
Depósito legal B. 27769-1978
Printed in Spain

I. INTRODUCTION

HOW THE CONQUEST WAS ACHIEVED AND THE LIFE OF ATAHUALPA

...Or how to conquer an empire with four dozen horses and a couple of hundred men.

Let us quickly run through the events of the conquest of Peru. Fransico Pizarro began by getting hold of an interpretor, Felipillo. (It is said that this Indian played an important part in the fall of the empire by betraying his own kind.) First a public relations campaign: the Spaniard billed and cooed winning speeches to the Indians, exchanged trinkets for gold, fresh water and game... Prudence and smiles were the order of the day.

Before landing at Tumbez, the first town he came to, the conquistador sent forth emissaries They were given the explicit order to touch nothing, even the most tempting objects, and to respect the inhabitants.

Pizarro then went back to Spain, where, before undertaking the conquest itself, he had himself named "Life Governor and Captain General of New Castille". It was then that the "conqista" began. From Panama, Pizarro set off again for Tumbez. But forced to land in bad weather, he sacked the first village he came to: methods had taken a definite turn, as this was only the first of a countless series of massacres. Skilfully playing off one tribe against another, attacking the Incas' enemies to curry favout with them, and taking advantage of the civil war between Huascar and Atahualpa, Pizarro made his way to near Cajamarca, where Atahualpa awaited him.

Many have tried to explain why the Inca chief fell into a trap and was taken prisoner. Did he believe what the men with beards, riding on animals that he had never seen, said? (Some claim it was the horse that conquered Peru.) Was he impressed, he who had never seen writing, by a book, the Bible, that was given to him before the attack? Did it fall from his hands, or did he throw it away, as the Spaniards claimed, seeing in this act the justification for all their excesses? Or, as John Hemming, a specialist on the conquest, has rightly supposed, did he underestimate the enemy, which, in heavy armour, on horseback and well-armed found it easy against the Indians in their tunics. One single Spaniard was wounded, while hundreds of natives died. There is no lack of explanations, but the reality is sad: Atahualpa accepted to pay a fabulous ransom, which did not prevent him being executed. He was forced to become a Christian at the end, to avoid perishing in the flames. In fact he thought that death by fire was the only way he could be prevented from coming back among his own people.

Atahualpa was strangled. And if Indian legends are to be believed, though he has not yet returned to the high Andean plateau to the sound of a flute and under the wings of a condor, then he will come... perhaps.

Left, a gate at Machu Picchu.
Opposite, a warrior's head.

THE BEGINNINGS OF THE INCA EMPIRE

At the death of Atahualpa, the Inca empire, then being conquered, included Peru, Ecuador and Bolivia, as well as territory now belonging to Colombia, Argentina and Chile.

It stretched mainly over four strips of parallel land running from North to South. First there was the sandy, inhospitable zone, which ran along the coast and was crossed by short rivers. This is where the Spaniards discovered the first villages, built of *adobe* (bricks of unbaked earth) on desert lands. Then there was the wide strip of the western Cordillera, which lies between 5,000 and 10,000 feet. Further inland there was the interandean plateau and the eastern Cordillera which constitutes a barrier facing the Amazonian forest. Four gigantic ribbons of earth between the ocean and the forest. "At one time there were only mofuntains and rock faces covered with brambles and thorns. Men were beasts without government, religion or permanent homes. They fed on grass, roots, wild fruits and often even human flesh. Those who were not continually naked covered themselves with animal pelts, tree bark or leaves. They took no other woman than the first one they met." This is how the Incas told the beginnings of their history to the Andean populations, at least if Garcilaso de la Vega the half Indian, half Spanish chronicler, born in Cuzco and who died in Cordoba, is to be believed. And they could have added: and then the Incas came. The word *Inca* means "chief" and was originally only used for the emperor. *Manco Capac* founded the dynasty. To assert his power, he claimed to be the son of the Sun. His origins went back to the 12th century. However, it was not until the 15th century that the Inca *Pachacuti* (the 9th of 12 emperors) gave the Inca empire the impetus for its rapid and impressive expansion.

The appearance of *Manco Capac* and the Incas stems from several legends. Manco and his wife (whom one supposes to have been her own mother as well) were begat by the sun god or came out of the waters of Lake Titicaca. Chroniclers have left descriptions of the lands from which they came. On the other hand, there are good reasons to believe that the *Quechuas*, are, as their language indicates, the original Incas. They lived with the *Aymares* on the Andean plateau.

PRE-INCAN CIVILIZATIONS

Men have lived in the region stretching from the Andean valleys to the Pacific for more than ten thousand years, in groups of hunters or fishermen, turning gradually to agriculture. The patient excavations which followed the discoveries of the German archeologist Max Uhle, have brought to light some of their tools and showed where their camp sites were. In the fourth millenary before our era, they settled mainly along the banks of rivers which crossed the arid coastal strip, and these rivers allowed them to live.

Little by little they grouped into villages and, although pottery made its appearance in the second millenary, life did not really change until the discovery of corn, towards the fifth century of our era. The development of the people living in the interior is less well known, although it is supposed to have been practically the same. However, it was on the plateau that textiles made their appearance, marking a definitive milestone. In effect, it is from this moment on that the Andean populations took over from those on the coast.

The most important of the interior civilizations seems to have been the *Chavin*. It stretched across the whole of the first millenary which preceded our era and was characterized by a ideological and religious unification, probably forced on it by

priests who lived in the *Huantar*. It is mainly through sculptures that have been discovered that we know them... badly. How can we ever explain or interpret the complicated lines on their bas-reliefs?

Mention should be made of three coastal civilizations that came after the Chavin and which reached right down to our era: the *Paracas-Nazca*, whose marvellous cloths were buried with the dead in the necropolis and were preserved to reveal their designs and colours; the *Mochicas*, who were followed by the *Chimus*, situated in northeast Peru and who left us one of the most extraordinary series of pottery ever; and the *Uros*, inveterate fishermen who settled on the strip of land that went down from Titicaca to the Pacific. Far from being barbarians, the *Chimus*, whose kingdom was already of a certain significance around the year 1000, were subdued by the Incas in 1476. The latter made great use of their traditions and arts. Among other things, they copied from them the habit of piercing the ears of noblemen.

It was on the plateau however that the *Aymaras* civilization flourished between about 900 and 1300 and it was only gradually integrated into the Empire. Their spoken language still survives in a large part of Bolivia, having resisted the pressures of Quechuan and Spanish. There are also ruins which allow us to make certain guesses about them. Their capital can be still visited today, the impress-

Priceless drawings of the time (they were made immediately after the Spanish Conquest), which can be found throughout this book and were done by Poma de Ayala. His self-portrait can be seen on the left. On the right, stones dating from before the Christian era (Lima Museum).

languages and customs up until the arrival of the Spaniards.

A HISTORY DIFFICULT TO TRACE

We quickly come to realize that what we know about pre-Incan civilizations has been provided for us by archeologists and is limited to a few certainties along with a lot of guesses. The same applies to the Incan civilization itself, described with so much imagination but so little objectiveness by the chroniclers. The Incas did not know how to write. Whom then can we trust? Of the oral traditions that have come down to us, many disagree. There is much legend. *Quipus* (knotted strings) provide us with figures that we have yet to interpret.

What the chroniclers wrote is often enchanting, such as the stories of *Poma de Ayala*, famous mainly for his drawings, which illustrate this book, or those of *Garcilaso de la Vega*, whom we have already mentioned—they were both of Indian mothers—or the numerous notes of the Conquistadores, inasmuch as they were able to observe the world that they were invading. But these reports are often so confusing and differ so much, that we can only guess at the real truth.

This is why Louis Baudin, an Inca specialist, even puts the existence of the first of the emperors in question in his latest book: "Although his statue is on the main square in Lima... *Manco Capac* perhaps never existed... It is also probable that his successor, *Sinchi Roca* was a compound of a whole line of chiefs, as the word *Sinchi* means a permanent chief." It is certain that at least as far down as the first emperors, history and myth are mingled. It is only with the Inca *Pachacuti* (circa 1438 to circa 1471), the greatest of conquerors, law-maker, administrator and builder rather than warrior (and even poet, if the chronicler Sarmiento is to be believed) that history starts to take shape, less than a century before the death of his great grandson Atahualpa. But we do know that under *Yahuar Huapac*, the 7th of 12 emperors, the Incas conquered the inhabitants ot the valley of Cuzco and that from there, expeditions and conquests continued under *Viracocha*, mainly *Pachacuti*, *Tupac Yuapanqui*, gradually turning an insignificant mountain tribe into one of the greatest empires of pre-Colombian America. It was the latter ruler's grandsons who waged a bloody war over the empire's succession, making the Spaniards' task easier.

ive *Tihuanaco*, near Lake Titicaca. The main attraction is the Sun gate and the giant statues. The *Aymaras* contributed a certain amount of useful knowledge to the Empire, such as the alloying of copper and tin. They also brought with them their *ayllu*, or system of family and economic organization though this was slightly modified afterwards.

As to the *Huari* civilization, it had its centre in the Mantaro valley, a region near where the Inca nation was founded. Contrary to the *Aymaras*, the *Huaris* spread their influence north. They unified neighbouring civilizations in regions as far as Cajamarca, imposing for example a style of pottery that directly influenced that of the Incas.

The *Aymara*, *Huari* and *Chimu* civilizations influenced each other. During the final centuries before the Inca invasion, their peoples built great cities. The *Chanchan* ruins, near the present town of Trujillo, cover a surface of 12 square miles. They were then "builders of cities" who were subdued by the Incas during the second half of the fifteenth century. However they preserved their

All types of climate are to be found in Peru, as can be seen on this double page of photos. Top left, a landscape on the north coast and, below, a view of the famous Lake Titicaca; opposite, a shot of the high plateau (14,000 feet); above, the astonishing site of Machu Picchu.

15

II. SOCIETY AND ITS ORGANIZATION

If its history is a puzzle to us, we can however exactly reconstruct what Inca society was. It can be broadly subdivided into two main classes that Louis Baudin has called the "elite" and the "masses". Going into detail, we can say that it was organized pyramid-fashion with the emperor at its head—*Sapa Inca* (or unique chief)—seconded by a "supreme council" made up of four "perfect ones", each of whom was responsible for one quarter of the kingdom. They were generally chosen from among the emperor's close relatives and their duties were not hereditary. Immediately below came the numerous members of the royal dynasty. "They were distinguished by several very important privileges, and wore special clothing... Most of them lived at court, near the prince, taking part in his councils, eating at his table and fed at his expense. They were the only ones allowed to acceed to the great sacerdotal duties. They were responsible for the control of the army and far-off garrisons, were put in charge of provinces and in a word occupied the positions of trust" (William Prescott).

They had under their orders the ex-chiefs of the subdued regions, who had become leading civil servants—the *curacas*. By keeping them in their jobs, the Incas skilfully managed to gain their trust, although they belonged to other tribes. It is true that they were forced to go to Cuzco periodically where their sons were made to study from 15 years old onwards, and were therefore subjected to a double control. The *curacas*, who were also chiefs of collectives or *ayllus*, had the duty to divide up land, to organize work sharing and to arbitrate on differences that arose within the *ayllu*, in principle according to local custom. In a word, they were commissioned to attend to the continuing life of the community.

As to the rest of the population, it was made up of the masses or the people. We will see in detail how life was organized. It can be simply said that if there was room for a certain individuality among the upper classes, then life was essentially a community existence for the lower ranks. If the members of the elite had inalienable rights that could be passed down by heredity, the masses had only one right: to work for the Inca, produce and reproduce for the Inca. In return he gave them the necessities of daily life, and if happiness was not available then at least there was peace, which was in sharp contrast to the harsh rule and terror to which they were submitted after the conquest.

On the left, the remains of an Inca fortress above Cuzco. Below, a typical Peruvian, unchanged since the Incas' time.

Left, a Peruvian woman. Above, an Inca statuette.
Below, a peasant on the banks of Lake Titicaca.

Above left, the Inca leads his troops to the front. Right, an officer presents the sovereign with the head of an enemy chief. Below, the Inca returns to the capital after a victory. Right, the absolute ruler with the empress on a palanquin. Opposite right, an imperial crown in solid gold.

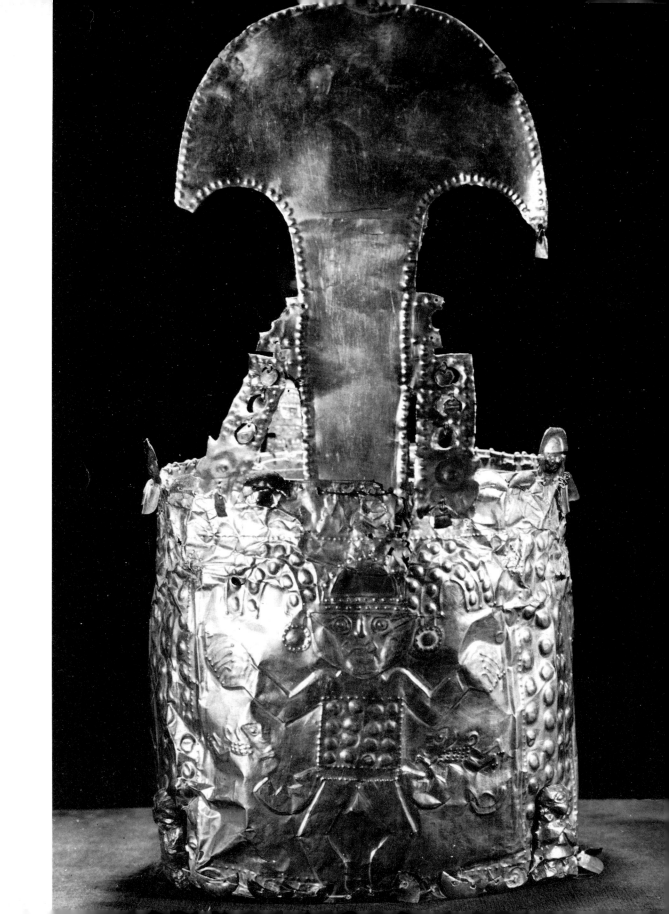

III. FAMILY LIFE

THE AYLLU

Borrowed from the *Aymaras* as we have seen and existing at every level of society, the *ayllu* was a sort of family clan living in economic self-sufficiency. In this respect it had developed since the time of the *Aymaras* for whom relationship was not a determining factor. For them it was more of a territorial union than a blood tie and an economic association. The Incas adopted the principle, but kept foreigners out. Each *ayllu* was then a collectivity with a common ancestor. For the mass of the people, it consisted mainly of farming communities formed into a *marca*, a piece of indivisible land belonging to the clan. Each *ayllu* occupied a village or a clearly defined section of a town. It could be relatively small and include only about 50 members, or count several hundreds. There were duties attached to belonging to an *ayllu*, but there were advantages as well, such as organized labour with proper work-sharing.

Inside the *ayllu*, which was the basic unit of the Andean society, there was a real feeling of solidarity. Everyone pulled together, especially when it was sowing or reaping time; widows and sick were helped, and their land looked after; together the men built the houses for newly-weds.

BLOOD TIES

The Incas had a system of parallel consanguinity that might seem strange to us: effectively, inside the *ayllu* there was a male line and a female line, that is, men were, it appears, descended from their fathers only and women from their mother. As to the family itself, it was obviously much more restricted than the community and much closer-knit. However, the names given to its different members were not the same if they originated from men or women. Thus a mother gave her children of different sexes the same name while the father distinguished the son from the daughter, but also used the word "son" for other relations such as nephews! The terms brother and sister were often used for first cousins. The Indians even used the words "father", "mother", "brother" or "sister" for all kinds of relations. This explains why there was so much confusion and why we don't have to take chroniclers too seriously when they claim that the supreme Inca, for example, married his own sister.

Left, décorative motifs from the Santas culture. Right, a curious Mochica vase.

LOVE AND MARRIAGE

In each Indian cottage there were children who one day came to love each other.

Love, in a society founded on the concept of work and geared to production rather than pleasure, where survival in the difficult climatic conditions that we know of was not always guaranteed, love then was the equivalent of marriage. Marriage established the union of strengths rather than that of hearts. The Indians eschewed romance. The young couple was under surveillance by the parents who had agreed to their union and young couples undertook "trial marriages" that lasted a few days or several years.

Furthermore, this marriage was mandatory and the upper age limit was thirty years old. Therefore, a man had to find a wife who worked as hard as possible and a woman had to find a husband with a bearable character. Virginity was of no value to the young peasants. In certain regions it was even a mark of dishonour, a virgin being a person who could please nobody. As to the "test marriage", even if it did not succeed, then it in no way affected reputation, much to the contrary. If children were born of this pre-matrimonial union, they were taken over by the mother's parents, who saw in them

extra pairs of hands for the future rather than extra mouths to feed. In addition, the Inca took care that they did not go hungry. The interest that others showed or had shown in the woman whom an Indian had chosen only made him more excited by her.

As to marriage itself, it gave the young man independence from his father and the right to own his own cottage, and plot of land, and to get hired help.

If polygamy was allowed, then it was to be found only among the leaders, the lower classes had enough on their hands with family, house and land. A marriage was in principle insoluble.

WEDDINGS

Weddings were officiated by a civil servant or *curaca* representing the supreme Inca and were carried out on a set day, once a year. The young boys and girls were brought together on the main squares of towns and villages and lined up in two ranks. The minimum age was 24 for the men and 18 for the girls. The *curaca* joined the hands of the different couples and declared them man and wife. He acted as judge if there was a dispute and had to decide who had the right to a woman coveted

*Intimitate love
in Mochica art.*

by several men.

"No man could choose a woman from outside the community to which he belonged" (Prescott). However, close relatives could not be chosen either. Only the sovereign could break the rules of the nation.

Noblemen and officials, by their more favourable situation, were, like the supreme Inca, often polygamous. However, they were married to a legitimate spouse whom they were not allowed to repudiate. During the weedding ceremony, and following the example set by the Inca, the representative of the upper classes put a finely decorated sandal symbolically onto the right foot of his fiancée and offered her presents. There was a sumptuous procession through carpeted streets for the Inca's wedding, sacrifices—of white llamas, among other things—and offerings.

The wedding day was a national holiday. The ceremonies, be they simple or elaborate—they changed not only by class but by region—were followed by meals to which close relatives were invited and ended in jollity and drunkenness.

Opposite, a young couple in bed.

THE BIRTH OF A LITTLE INDIAN

If marriage was mandatory—or celibacy not allowed—it was because its role was essential to the continuity of the race. The Empire could not afford to be short of labour to cultivate the soil or to carry on wars. Birth then was considered as a welcome phenomenon—over which the people had little time to linger—and a woman who gave birth to twins was promoted to the rank of "sacred".

The Indian woman gave birth wherever she happened to be and almost without pain as she worked right up to the end. She herself cut the umbilical cord and took the infant to the nearest stream where she washed it, first putting the water into her mouth to warm it. Once hers and the child's toilet were finished, she put the child into a light cot specially prepared for it, where it stayed without moving for the first months. One of the rules which governed the most intimate parts of an Indian's life forbade him to take an infant into his arms, so that the baby would not get used to tenderness and that there would be no risk of the child getting what it wanted by tears or screams. Carried about everywhere in its cot, the baby did not get in the way of work. To feed it, the mother knelt by the cot and leaned over it. Breast feeding could only take place three times a day.

At a year old or more, the baby was given a provisional name, which recalled the circumstances of its birth, such as "fine sand", or "storm rain" or "closed fist". When it became too big to remain swathed a hole was dug for it in the ground and lined with cloth. Here it learnt to walk and climb. Weaning took place at about the age of two.

THE LIFE OF A MAN

The Incas, with their extremely developed sense of organization, distinguished the various phases of existence. The first period was that of the "child in the cot" and lasted until about two years old. It was the parents, naturally, who looked after the baby, sharing its first games and taking care that it didn't fall or burn itself. The second period went up until the age of five. The child was still free to play, to be excited by its top or domestic animals. Then up until nine, games gave way slowly to education based mainly on the parents' example. "It was important that the child be educated and punished for the good of the kingdom", Poma de Ayala wrote.

From nine onwards, the boy made himself useful by hunting birds that were a menace to fields and crops. From 12 to 18, he looked after the herds of llamas and caught the brightly-couloured birds whose feathers the *curaca* was fond of. He learned his first crafts. The period up to his twentieth birthday was marked by abstinence and poverty and he had no right yet to love. Although at 20 he began to carry out all his tasks alone, it was only from the age of 25 that he was considered as a fully-fledged subject of the Empire and was recorded as such in statistics.

From 25 onwards, the Indian had the right to a slower pace of work and could no longer be drafted. He was however obliged to serve according to his capacity and strength. If the chroniclers are to be believed, it was only between 80 and 100 years old, that "old, hard of hearing, and just able to eat and sleep, to plait ropes, breed rabbits and ducks", he had the right to a certain amount of rest and respect.

As to the sick, deaf, dumb, blind, hunchbacked, dwarves etc., they did the jobs that their handicaps allowed and they were married, believe it or not, to the sick, deaf, dumb, hunchbacked, stunted etc. Obviously, the state had thought of everything.

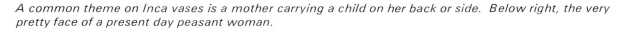

A common theme on Inca vases is a mother carrying a child on her back or side. Below right, the very pretty face of a present day peasant woman.

AND WHAT ABOUT GIRLS AND WOMEN?

A girl's life began like a boy's but was directed early on to a specific future role. Thus she looked after her junior brother, worked near the hearth or picked flowers. From 12 years old, all her hair was removed, hence the name of "little cropped one". In a short skirt and barefoot, she learnt the art of cooking, spinning and weaving and of making *chicha*, an alcoholic drink. Considered immature for intimate relations, she remained chaste under penalty of death. At 18, of a marriageable age, her life changed, and though none of her work was spared her, she had a certain sexual freedom, which was relative according to regions, and which ended with marriage. In fact, adultery was considered as a crime and punished by death.

And woman? Prematurely aged, considered by man—and this was valid for all levels of society with a few nuances—as an object, "seeming to belong" according to Baudin, "to a class halfway between human and thing", having less rights within her cottage than domestic animals, she soon became very unattractive. True, she was not badly treated, but neither were the llamas or guinea pigs. And though its importance was recognized, even her reproductive function was hardly respected.

Her life was even more strictly regimented than man's. For instance, chastity was forced on her again if she was widowed at a certain age. She was taught to work uninterupted at continuous profitability. She had to spin while walking and chew corn as soon as she stopped. She finished the day delousing children, while she did not even have time to get rid of her own parasites.

Furthermore, at an early age, a girl stood a good chance of being picked by the Inca's inspectors to become a "Sun Virgin", like a noble's daughter, or of being offered as a present to a meretitious civil servant, and whoever he may have been, it was not a very enviable position.

GROWING-UP CEREMONIES

Two main ceremonies marked a child's life. The first celebrated a kind of official joining of the *ayllu* and included the first cutting of his hair and nails. It was a godfather, chosen by the parents, who began, using a flint for cutting that he then

29

Left, present day peasant women in the high plateau. Above and below, Indians in a Cuzco street.

passed to the other members of the family. The nails and hair were then carefully kept because of the belief in their magic power. Effectively, if a third person took them, he was considered to have taken a part of the child's personality, acquiring an influence over him to which he had no right.

The second festival again united the whole family. It took place for the boy at the age of puberty, and for the girl at the time of her first period—between 12 and 14 years old, according to the region. For the boy it represented his incorporation into the nation. His legs were whipped, he was recalled his duty towards his parents and chiefs, and then he was given the *huara*, a sort of loincloth. It was also at this festival that he was given his final name, which was made up of two parts: one generic, directly linked to the *ayllu*, the other personal, connected to the child itself, to its merits or certain circumstances of its life. The young girl made great preparation for a similar ceremony, during which she was also given her name.

SCHOOLS OR THE EDUCATION OF NOBLEMEN

Science was not intended for the people and this was the Inca's direct wish. Tupac Yuapanqui declared that it only "bloated and made vain and arrogant those of lower rank". The one and simple aim of the education of the lower classes was to make them a working tool in the government's and community's service. It was different for the members of the imperial *ayllu* (the descendants of each emperor belonged to a different *ayllu*) or for the sons of *curacas*. Schools were there for these people only.

Lessons were given by *amautas*, whose name meant "wise men", as they were capable of filling the roles of architect, lawyer, artist or teacher. Education depended on the child's rank and the function he was intended to fill afterwards. Schooling finished with a sort of exam or *huaracu*, which was both a test and an initiation.

STRICT TEACHING

It was at about the age of 15 that studies began and lasted for four years. The first part was

32

mainly taken up with study of *Quechua* or the official language, the second with religion, the third with *quipus,* which were used for census taking, statistics etc, and the fourth covered the history of the kingdom. Geometry, geography and astronomy were also touched on.

Teaching was, it goes without saying, of a strict nature. Masters taught knowledge that was not to be questioned. Corporal punishment however was not used, except for smacks under the feet, once a day if necessary for laziness or disobedience.

Physical exercises played an important part in education and were also tested in the *huaracu.*

The tests of this final exam, which were prepared at length, were followed with enthusiasm and anxiety by the contestant's family. They included, among other things, a race, a group combat, archery, catapult handling, and technical tests, such as making weapons or sandals. If sanctions, at least direct ones, were not taken against poor contestants (who were however open to public mockery, after the race, for instance), successful candidates were received by the *Sapa Inca* in person, who gave them prizes of clothing but mainly pierced their ears, giving them the right to wear heavy earrings which were the distinctive sign of the upper class and which earned them the Spanish name of *orejones* (big ears).

Left, vase in a human shape (Chicago Museum, the Nathan Cummings Collection). Below left, an Inca chief and his child: the drawing is very realistic. Right, deformed ears, which were a particularity in Inca noblemen.

IV. DRESS, ORNAMENTS, BODY CARE

UTILITY CLOTHING

The State provided clothing for the whole of the people. Strictly controlled, simple and uniform, clothing left no room for coquetry and imagination. It was purely utilitarian. On the other hand, the Indians were not afraid of nudity and covered themselves only against the cold. Arms and legs were exposed to the often icy air of the Cordillera.

It was on the wedding day that they got from the civil servants what was to act as long as possible as clothing. Bride and groom had the right to two suits in llama wool, one for holidays, the other for work. These clothes lasted until they fell to pieces. They had to be skilfully sewn and repaired a hundred times before they dared ask for new ones. They were all cut from the same model, a little lighter in colour for women than for men and no modifications could be made without the express approval of the civil servant responsible.

The man wore a kind of white, sleeveless shirt, the *uncu*, a loincloth, the *huara*, a strip of cloth that passed between his legs and was held at the waist by a woollen rope. He threw a cape or brown poncho over his shoulders. The woman for her part, wore a long tunic, split at the sides to allow her to walk more easily, the *anaco*, held at the waist by a belt. Her dress was also completed by a shawl of woven wool, the *liclla*, held on her breast by a large pin or *topo*.

The peasants worked barefoot. It was only when they travelled or when they wore holiday clothes that they put on sandals, called *ojotas*, made with the thickest part of a llama's skin. The sole however did not protect the underside of the foot. It left the toe free for the Indian to cling to uneven terrain if he slipped. The sandal was attached to the foot by a woollen cord.

A LITTLE MORE REFINEMENT

The clothes of civil servants, nobles and the Inca himself were not of a different model, but were of a finer weave and often dyed with iridescent colours and covered with geometric designs as Poma de Ayala's drawings show. Vicuna wool was mostly used for the Emperor. The *orejones* always wore sandals on their feet, the first of which was solemnly given to them the day they were admitted into this social order.

The Inca wore the *llantu*, the insignia of his

Left, embroidered cloth of the Paracas culture. Above, a present day peasant woman wearing a poncho: the decorative designs are the same as in Inca times.

35

supreme power. It was a multi-coloured plait rolled several times round his head and from which hung the *marcapaicha*, a fringe of tassels and with two *coraquenque* feathers, a very rare bird whose plumage was exclusively reserved to make the royal head-gear. Noblemen's hair was short and their ears stretched under the weight of their earrings. On their head they wore various decorations representative of the region they came from.

In addition, the Inca had his kness and ankles bound with ribbons.

As to the empress—the *coya*— her dress was distinguished by its colours and designs. The large-headed pin which crossed her breast was, needless to say, of great value. Her long hair, covered with a fine cloth, hung down her back, while her suite only had the right to a ribbon around their head.

Left, detail of a llama wool cape (Lima Museum). Below, ornaments on a cloth (Paracas culture).
On the following pages: a personage from ancient times (vase) and a present day woman, both squatting.

seen, rather unattractive. She stopped taking care of herself, neglecting even to mend the holes in her clothing, which she closed up as best she could with pins.

Oral hygiene occupied the inhabitants of the Empire somewhat more and they generally had beautiful, healthy teeth. They rubbed their gums with boiling-hot herbs bringing on irritations that prevented them from eating anything for several days. But once the dead skin disappeared, what pride they had in showing shining red gums, that were splendid to their eyes.

Facing, golden hair remover (Mochica civilization). Below, an Inca chief's golden ornament (Bogota Gold Museum).

BODY CARE

Although the *coya* took great care of her hair, as a drawing of Poma de Ayala's shows, neither man nor woman of the people had much time for their toilet. Their skin, tanned by the wind and sun, bore all weathers. They did not wash regularly, and were not worried by what we would call "lack of hygiene", which to them was only a "natural state".

The man generally made do with combing himself. The woman, mainly before her marriage and up to her first child, washed her linen and rubbed it with stinging leaves. She took time choosing her *topo* and softened her hair by washing it in her own urine. Her comb was made of cactus spines. Sometimes she even bothered to remove her hair with a paste made of ashes and heated urine.

But if the man maintained a certain appeal, hard work soon got the better of feminine coquetry and the Indian women ended by being, as we have

DIFFERING HAIRSTYLES

Although clothing was uniform it was not the same with hairstyles and head-gear. Men in the capital wore their hair short, while in the provinces, the length varied according to local custom. Lower class women generally plaited their hair and tied it with ribbons.

The variety of hairstyles had a more practical than aesthetic function. It had been decided that the Indian would live and die at the place of his birth, and he travelled only to go to a neighbouring market or to make a pilgrimage. But he could also be drafted or called to take part in the great works of the Empire, such as building of roads or temples or mining. It was easy for the Inca's inspectors to recognize each man and identify his place of origin (to keep the census up to date) thanks to the hairstyles.

Each region or province had then its own head-gear or special hairstyle, and even here little fantasy was allowed. The *Canchas* wore a black and red band on their forehead, the *Collas* a woollen bonnet, the *Canaris* a kind of wooden crown, while the *Huancas* simply made themselves short plaits.

The remains of the "Inca bath", 15 miles from Cuzco.

V. FOOD

BASIC PRODUCTS

In surroundings that were hardly made to man's dimension and which served as a background to the Indian's daily life, vegetable came before animal, at least where food was concerned. The llama, which was only eaten occasionally, was mainly the children's inseperable companion and a provider of wool. The other camelidae, such as the vicuna and the guanaco, were not domesticated. They could only be captured on the Inca's orders. Other pets, such as dogs and guinea pigs, played a secondary role in the diet.

The peasant lived mostly on the products of his fields, Beside potatoes and corn, he ate a kind of rice, *quinua,* and several kinds of dry vegetables such as *canahua,* which grew at more than 12,000 feet high, or certain varieties of dry beans, all abundantly seasoned with *aji* or "Indian pepper", according to the Spaniards. In more exotic areas, the tomato was known and certain fruits such as the pineapple, the banana, *guabas* and *chirimoyas.*

PRESERVES

Andean populations rarely ate fresh products. Crops had to be shared to last for 12 months. This is why preserves were of great importance. Corn and ground *quinua* provided flour and semolina. They were crushed on concave stones, using smaller half-moon shaped blocks.

Potatoes were the base for *chuño,* a sort of dry paste made by methods that can still be seen today on the high Bolivian plateau. Women stand on little heaps of fecula and with a skill and patience that seems endless they press them and move their feet for days on end. The mass dries under the combined action of the sun and the cold nights.

Great quantities of various herbs were also preserved. Llama and guinea pig meat could be salted and dried to give *charqui,* that was cut into thin strips.

Added to these products were dried snails, the fruit of certain varieties of cactus, frogs, worms,

mushrooms, and in marine or lake areas, certain types of fish or sea food.

The method of preserving was simple. The products were placed in clay pots or small boxes made from corn stems, with large quantities of *muña.* This is a plant of the mint family with insect killing properties. The pots and boxes—made of lattice work in humid areas—were kept in cavities in the cottage roof or in the earth. In dry regions, the food was carefully wrapped with a layer of straw before burying.

Chicha, the alcoholic drink that the Indians liked so much, was made with two of the types of corn known at that time. It was made in the cottages throughout the year and was no different from the kind that is drunk today. In ancient Peru it was mainly women (mostly old women)—when they had a moment's respite—who took care of it. They chewed conn seeds and spat the paste they obtained into a pan of water, which was then sealed and buried. Time, heat and saliva helping, fermented the liquid.

MEALS

Indian meals were frugal, obviously more by necessity than taste. This could be seen at banquets where no reserve was called for: everybody tucked in joyfully. Was the peasant's daily diet sufficient? It seems that fats and proteins taken were hardly enough and that the calory count was low, which explains the Indian's passion for spices and *chicha.* However, Louis Vacarel, a Peruvian historian and ethnologist says: "The diet was reasonable and deteriorated a lot after the conquest."

Food was prepared on a clay hearth at the centre of the room using terra cotta pots. Fires were lit by rubbing two pieces of wood together. The two main meals were at nine o'clock in the morning and between four and five in the afternoon. The wife filled the plates which she placed on the ground, then crouched on her haunches next to her husband; they leaned against each other back to back. And even if the animals which surrounded them were to help themselves from their master's plate, it would have been highly improper for the wife to do the same.

Meals were made up of a soup into which a few fresh vegetables were thrown and *chuño* or rice, accompanied by corn. This was eaten in all kinds of ways: cooked, grilled, smoked, in semolina, etc. If they felt like an extra dish, the family indulged in

This vase, found in the coastal region of Peru, shows a person holding a recipient.

Left, a dish decorated with two fishes. Right, a vase in gold (Chimu civilization) and a gourd made from a dried pumpkin.

the luxury of snails, one or two worms or a bamboo shoot. Llama meat was not dried and was eaten only on holidays. The young ate it raw, hoping that by doing so they would increase their strength.

Although people ate little in Peru, they drank a lot. Alcohol was liked and drinking sessions frequent, mainly, of course during holidays. Guests brought their own food; everyone sat on the ground in two rows, presided by a civil servant, who had the right to a seat. The Indians then drank themselves stupid with calm and dignity as if their act was part of a religious service.

Not only the Indians like *chicha;* there was also a weakness for it in the imperial palace.

Noblemen's food was naturally richer and more varied. The Inca himself took three meals a day. They were made up of tropical fruits, fresh meat of young llamas or vicunas, fish, wild duck... It was served in turn by his wives, who were assisted by servants. He was shown different dishes from which he made his choice. The "duty" wife held up the gold or earthenware plates at the right height so that the monarch could eat without bending forward. When he had finished, the remains were put into coffers and burnt so that no one would be tempted to touch them.

VI. HABITAT

THE INDIAN HUT

We have already mentioned the hut to which the young married couple had the right and which later sheltered animals and children. It was generally made up of one room where everyone lived, although this depended on the region.

The climate on the coast was temperate because of the Humboldt current. Little rain fell from an often cloudy sky. The houses, which were built less solidly than inland, had windows at the time of the Incas, for airing purposes. They were rectangular and made of bricks with a straw roof, which was pointed and sometimes came over the roof to make to make a porch that was held up on little columns.

On the high plateau the climate was much tougher, the temperature changed a lot during the day and torrential and violent rains fell. The hut was therefore very different. The walls were of stone or *adobe* with no opening to the outside; this gave the little houses the look of identical blocks. The buildings were mainly intended to protect from the cold and damp. The *adobes* used were much bigger than the bricks we know today. They were made of clay with twigs and pieces of bamboo which gave them a greater resistance to the weather.

The huts were generally circular and had neither fireplace nor window. There was an opening at ground level, as small as possible to allow entry on all fours. Inside, the visitor was surprised by the heat and dark. The walls were generally less than four feet high and were covered, under the thatching, with soot and grease. The smell of meals and animals—they often left their droppings—and smoke filled the air. The Indians, however, did not seem to be disturbed by it. Spanish missionaries on the other hand have left us horror-struck reports.

Kitchen utensils were left all around the main hearth. Clothing hung from the roof or was piled into jars, often the only "furniture". People slept on the ground in a woollen square or llama skin, which acted as blanket and mattress.

In some huts a sort of screen separated the place where clothing and food were kept from the rest of the room. Recesses were made in the walls. Knives and spoons, as well as figurines belonging to the

Upper left, a peasant hut in the Peruvian high plateau. Below, evocation of an Inca house. Below opposite, decorative design on a jar, showing a veranda.

family cult, were kept there, along with other utensils. At home, the Indians generally sat on their haunches, feet together and chin on their knees. Those who were not so poor had a bench of stone or bricks in front of the house.

All ornamentation was forbidden and an inspector made a visit twice a year; his job was also to control the state of the house. However, he declined to go inside.

The home grew better as one went up the social ladder. Smalltime civil servants had maisonettes that were bigger and more hygienic. Noblemen had the right to several rooms, which were laid out around an interior courtyard. In the centre was a fountain. There were tapestries on the walls.

VILLAGES

The Andean population was divided into a host of small farming and pastoral communities. Villages in the mountain areas were sometimes situated at more than 12,000 feet high. There were other communities on the high plateau, or *puña,* which was over 14,000 feet high. The floors of the valleys, on the other hand, were thinly populated.

A promontory or summit was generally chosen for the site of a village, leaving free ground which was easier to cultivate. Furthermore, the site was easier to defend. The houses were not built according to a plan, but followed the contour of the land as much as possible. They sometimes spread over terraces or were grouped around a small square. These agglomerations could count as few as a dozen families or as many as several hundred.

The dominating colour of the villages was grey-green. Generally, there were neither wells nor water tanks, so that the women had to go several miles to the nearest stream or river for water.

Opposite and right, Inca remains on an island in Lake Titicaca. Facing, a chair of the Chavin time.

50

TOWNS

The Inca Pachacuti, great administrator and law-maker, as we have seen, was the originator of Andean urban planning. The major towns of the Empire were all built on the same model. Around a central square—where the public gathered for festivals and ceremonies—were a succession of public buildings, the chiefs' houses, silos, and pens where the lamas were kept. The streets, as narrow as in the villages, followed the terrain and often became stairs cut out of the rock. The buildings bore no decorations, in line with a taste for simplicity and from a necessity to resist the numerous earthquakes.

Among the major towns of the four provinces of the Empire, there was *Quito*, with its temple to the Sun and the Moon, *Cajamarca* and its great square, the scene of the encounter between Atahualpa and Pizarro, *Vilacamba*, isolated in the mountains, *Hatoun Colla*, on the banks of Lake

Titicaca, *Huamachuco*, at the crossroads of several main roads, *Tumbez*, the only sea port. Added to these were other towns with ruins that still impress tourists today: *Ollantaytambo*, source of legends, and the mysterious *Machu Pichu*, which we will speak of further.

We still do not know what was the population of these towns. However, it is thought that it did not exceed more than a few thousand. The Spaniards estimated the population of Cajamarca at two thousand. On the other hand, they thought Cuzco contained more than 200,000 people.

THE "NAVEL OF THE EARTH"

In Quechua, the name of the capital *Cuzco* meant "navel of the earth". Pachacuti built most of it.

Situated at 11,000 feet in a high valley, the town, because of the proximity of the tropics, had a climate that was healthy and good for farming. It was built by 50,000 Indians.

The centre of the town was a great gravel-covered square, where festivities took place. From it led roads to all four cardinal points. From the centre outwards were the different quarters which went in descending order of importance of inhabitants. Thus the poorest areas were on the outskirts. The poor quarters were dressed up with picturesque names such as "Salt Depot", "Talking Square"

Below, buildings in Machu Picchu. Right, a general view of Cuzco and a street in the city containing remains of Inca buildings.

(the Emperor's orders were given here), "Golden Serpent", or "Puma's Tail".

Among other things, the town owed its aspect to two streams, which were canalized and crossed with wooden bridges, of which one, the Huatanay, cut the main square into two esplanades. It was on one of these that the people gathered for important festivals. The other, closed on three sides by the walls of the imperial palace, looked more like a courtyard.

The predominant colour of the buildings was grey. As in other towns, massive buildings without ornamentation or sculpture, dominated the whole. In Cuzco, they held the "shadows" of dead emperors. In effect, at the death of each Inca, his palace was closed off. The new sovereign took over his own residence. The flagged streets were only wide enough for two or three persons and intersected each other at right angles. Along their middle, a gutter collected rain water.

There were four smaller squares where the inhabitants of the Empire came for the Sun festival. The great walls without openings behind which were the Emperor's apartments, impressed everybody. When visitors arrived they were installed in one of the four quarters of the town which corresponded to the region they came from. Civil servants could easily check the system by the different hairstyles.

Left and right, Inca walls which form the base of a college in Cuzco. Below, remains of the Inca palace in the capital.

VII. AGRICULTURE, FISHING AND HUNTING

POTATOES AND CORN

Inca society lived mainly by farming. Fields were farmed in common by members of a community. In accordance with the strict rules of the State, they were divided into three parts. The first plot went to the Sun god, that is to say, the crops raised on that land were used for rites and ceremonies. The second was set aside for the Inca, his family, servants and soldiers. The third was shared amongst the growers and members of the *ayllu*.

The types of soil were radically different according to their situation. There was little in common between the sands of the coastal region and the earth of the high plateau, between areas sheltered by forest and snow-covered fields. Most of the Indian population was concentrated in the sierra, which was crossed with deep valleys. Cultures were spread over their slopes and were conditioned by the climate. This is why the Andean economy has been called "vertical".

Two different kinds of production regulated life in the Empire: potato growing and llama breeding on the one hand, on the high plateau, and corn on the other, in lower regions. Most of reserves were made up of the latter.

It is said that the potato comes from the Andes. Developing its growth across the centuries, the Indians obtained seven hundred varieties, some of which grew above 18,000 feet high. The climate in the *puña* favoured the making of *chuño*, a potato-based product, that could be conserved for years.

In the highlands, cultures were subject to the influence of the rains, as irrigation was practically impossible at this altitude. The crops then varied according to the climatic conditions that they needed.

Corn was not as hardy as potatoes. It demanded a certain amount of water and would not stand such a rigourous climate. It could not be grown at more than 11,000 feet and at not less than 4,000, where the air became too dry. It required an irrigation system that was difficult to develop.

The slope of the land made such work difficult and a remedy was found by making terraces.

This plant, which in addition was used to make *chicha* and was supplied to many of the emperor's people, was considered good enough to be offered to the gods during ceremonies. It was even the basis for the Empire's survival.

Left, a Huancayo rural landscape. Right, a peasant.

TERRACE CULTURE

Terrace culture existed before the Incas came on the scene. But the emperors did all they could to encourage its development by stimulating the ingenuity and perseverance of the peasants. The mountains seemed to be made of gigantic stairways from the floor of the valley to the very peaks. Held up by walls that leaned slightly inwards in order to improve support of the banking, they followed the shape of the terrain for miles at a time.

The most fertile earth in the area was carried up by men or llamas. It was spread on a porous layer of gravel and sand and this system of drainage, designed to perfection, gave the soil just the right degree of moisture.

The hundreds of miles of irrigation systems still arouses our admiration even today. Water was brought from nearby glaciers by a system of underwater canals and aqueducts, which ensured regular moistening.

The earth used for potato growing had to be left fallow from time to time. So that the same did not have to be done with terrace cultures, the Incas introduced fertilizers which gave uninterupted corn crops. Human and animal excreta was collected. But *guano* was mostly used; this is bird droppings which accumulate on the *Chinchas* Islands, not far from the coast. These islands were called the "snow lands" because of their white aspect. By spreading the guano carefully, food was made available to every community.

HOW TO WORK THE EARTH

The Andean peasant knew how to get the best out of the hostile environment in which he lived. It is estimated that by grafting and selection, he managed to get 40 different products grown in the climatic levels of his country. Apart from corn and potatoes, he grew another cereal, *quinoa,* different varieties of beans, pimentoes, peanuts, gourds, avocado and cotton, to name only the most important ones. He also grew certain varieties of orchids, a rare flower, which to him was both medicine and sacred, and *coca,* the magic plant of the Andes, whose leaves are a stimulant and at the same time help fight hunger, thirst and pain.

The plots distributed to families included land situated at different altitudes to allow cultures of all kinds. The plot of land needed for one person's subsistence was called a *tupu.*

The peasants first cultivated the land reserved for the Sun and the Inca, then looked after the plots for the old, sick, widows and orphans or those who had been drafted. Finally, they worked their own land, without neglecting to help their neighbours on theirs.

Farming the Inca's lands was something of a festival. Dressed as if for a ceremony, the peasants were up at dawn to their chiefs' cries. Under the watchful eye of the men, the women and children went off to their alloted fields. The civil servants distributed the work and the men lined up with their wives in front of them. They began the work at one go, singing as they went.

The plough was unknown to the Incas and they used a simple instrument called the *taclla.* It was a piece of hard wood just over three feet long, the size of a stick or little stake, on which a sort of stock was fixed. A short piece of wood was also fixed to the lower part at a right angle for the peasant to push down on when he put the *taclla* into the soil. He then moved it back and forward to open the soil, which the women immediately broke up with their hands. They removed small stones and then sowed the soil. The presence of Indian women was not only for work purposes; they were supposed to possess supernatural powers. As

Left, a paring-knife in bronze. Centre, evocation of a peasant in a corn field. Below, ropes, agricultural instruments and wooden spade for digging the earth.

61

they were mothers they were believed to be in closer contact with Mother Earth than the men.

THE PEASANT'S CALENDAR

The official Inca calendar fixed the beginning of the year at December 21, the day of the Sun festival. For the peasant, however, it began with crop sowing.

It was in July that the work began on the Inca's lands and on those of the Sun. The earth was dug, and corn seeds were sown. First the community's lands were worked, then the family's. Potatoes were planted and there was plenty of work to do right up to September. It was then that the vegetable crop was picked as well as the spices that were intended for preserves. During times of drought, all methods were employed to invoke the help of the gods. October was partly set aside for searching for wood. Ropes were made, huts repaired. November and December were devoted to worship of the Sun god and veneration of the dead. During this time, preserves were the main food.

The new year began with a month dedicated to the Moon, or *Quilla* in Quechua. Then the fields were hoed and cleaned up. The children had to hunt birds with catapults, while women frightened them by beating on tambourines. It was a month when it rained a lot. Most of the time the families stayed in their cottages repairing their clothes. A lot of praying went on, and neither penance nor sacrifice was spared.

The second month (which was partly the equivalent of February) was that of hope. The coming crop could be felt. It was easy to remove the weeds from the fields because of the moisture in the soil. Canals and paths were mended.

The third month saw the corn sprout, after the children had protected it with all their might from the birds which loved to eat these tender plants.

Finally, in May, it was harvest time, flowers blooming and largesse. The whole family took part in the work, sorted the leaves, removed seeds from the ears, put the fruit into categories.

In June, potatoes were picked, immediately followed by *chuño* production.

Then, before resuming the soil's cycle, the peasants checked their huts, canals, paths and stores. Civil servants went around the country inspecting people and places, counting heads to prepare the next land-sharing.

PUBLIC STOREHOUSES AND SILOS

After the harvest, the surplus of cereals and the products from the Inca's and the Sun's lands were carried by man or llama to the public storehouses *(pirona)* and to the silos *(collca)*.

These were lined up through the town—well apart to lessen the fire risk—along country roads and in areas where drought was common. Storehouses and silos were watched by guards who were also storekeepers. These men checked and recorded deliveries and departures of goods with their *quipu*.

It was mainly seed that was stocked, cotton, wool and food supplies, which were used to feed the army, the clergy and the rich. Most of the foodstuffs however were kept exclusively in case of disasters, of which there was no shortage. If a community was victim of an earthquake, invasion or any calamity at all, it received the state's help. The surplus collected made up for the loss suffered.

So that every region got an equivalent share, goods were carried from the coast to the hills and vice versa. The Spaniards discovered reserves that would have been sufficient, according to them, to feed the population for ten years !

Among the ruined storehouses that can still be visited today, there is *Piki-Llacta*, 20 miles from Cuzco. Many buildings, almost a town, can be seen, with streets up to 20 feet wide. The llama pens alternated with silos and storehouses.

This well-designed system had however a major disadvantage. The spirit of thrift and care taken to the extreme made the Incas accumulate stocks until they went rotten, and finally much had to be thrown away.

BREEDING

The Andes was the only part of America in pre-Columbian times where systematic breeding was practised. The Incas domesticated two camelidae: the alpaca and the llama.

Here again, as for farming, goods were shared into three parts: one for the Sun, one for the emperor, and one for the *ayllu*. Llama breeding was the most important. This animal was common in the north of the Empire, especially around Lake Titicaca.

The State herds numbered 500 to 1000 heads each. Experienced shepherds were charged with

their care. Transhumance took place throughout the year, the herd staying at altitude as long as possible.

The number of beasts was continually checked and the shepherds had to follow strict rules. They were sorted and classified according to their sex, age and colour. Breeding was carefully controlled. Every town had its llama pen, and, although many of them were sacrificed, the females were never touched. The llama was mainly a beast of burden, although it could only carry small loads. This was made up for by sharing the weight among as many animals as possible. These caravans went slowly but surely. They spent the night in the open

could stand the climate of the high plateau.

The alpaca was not used for transport, but provided quality wool instead.

Pastures belonged to the community. They were vast fields which went up as far as the eternal snows. They could not be enclosed. Each family took whichever part it wanted from the common land and led its herd to pasture there.

Apart from the State and *ayllu* herds, there were also beasts belonging to families, on a private basis. They were kept by children and young people. They made little groups of from ten to a hundred animals, those possessing the most being the *curacas* and their families.

Drawings by Poma de Ayala of agricultural work during the different seasons. Left to right: in January, when it rained a lot, the earth was tilled. In February, the corn was tended to under cloudy skies. In March, a child and dog hunt birds in the fields during rainy weather. The April sun ripened the crops but... thieves had to be watched out for. Harvesting took place under the May sun. Potato picking was in June.

Below, from left to right: grain was put into the silos in July; chickens ate the leftovers. The bright August sun presided over sowing ceremonies, with men and women taking part. In September, when the weather was already breaking, the fields were tidied. October was the time when birds had to be kept away most of all. The earth was watered in November. December was right for a second sowing.

Two Indian peasant women with a llama. Right, a vase originating from the south coast.

THE LLAMA

With a circulatory system that could stand the highest altitudes, the "sheep of the Andes" was a sort of symbol in the Inca world. It was also called "camel of the clouds" or "heavenly horse".

It was the Indian's best friend. Even if its wool was of lesser quality than the alpaca's or the vicuna's, it was nevertheless used for ponchos and blankets. We also know the purpose its meat served. Its droppings were used for fuel and its leather to protect the traveller's feet. Its skin was made into blankets and even its bones were made into flutes by the Indians. The female was not milked as the Incas did not know the uses or value of milk. (The llama was probably a cross between the guanaco and the vicuna.) It could carry a load of 70 to 100 pounds and walk three to four leagues a day, feeding on what it found en route. Its digestive system, like that of the camel's, could stock abundant quantities of food and it could go without water for weeks. Its hooves, unlike those of the horse, were not hard but spongy, with a pointed heel that could grip the ice.

In principle the llama is a gentle and submissive animal. He will only refuse to go on when he is exhausted. The Indians treated it with affection and respect, understanding its sometimes irritable character. If angered, the llama spits green and foul-seling liquids.

We will discuss sacrifices later on, but it should be said that the llama saved many human lives. The priests always accepted the animal rather than an Indian, on condition that the animal bore the man's name!

The llama can be found everywhere, be it on the banks of Lake Titicaca or on the terraces of Machu Picchu. The vases and the drawings reproduced on this page are witness to the importance of the animal in rural life.

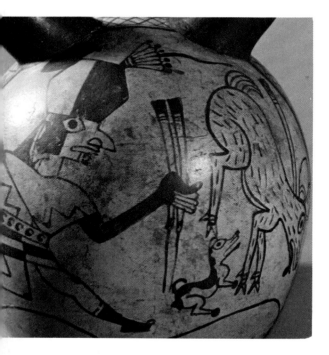 

HUNTING AND FISHING

On the other hand, the Indians never managed to tame the *guanaco* and the vicuna, from which they nevertheless took quantities of wool. These two animals roamed free in the mountains with only the condor for companion. The graceful vicuna, with its slit, almost human, eyes, had a coat as soft as down and provided the emperor's clothes. Moreover, it had been decided that these animals would belong exclusively to the reigning Inca. It was therefore forbidden to capture or kill them. Once a year, round-ups were organized superintended by the emperor and his closest officers. These hunts only took place once every four years on the same territory.

The operation took place as follows: all the inhabitants of the area—which sometimes meant up to 50,000 men—spread out in a gigantic circle. They herded in the game towards the centre, killing carnivorous animals as they went, slowly closing in on the vicunas and guanacos. They slaughtered a few males which could be used for

skin and meat. Then the females were caught—up to 40,000—and they were all shorn before being released. Afterwards the wool was given to the Sun Virgins who spun and wove it to make material as soft as silk.

There was plenty of fish in the Pacific and Lake Titicaca. Hooks, nets and traps were used. The Indians sailed Lake Titicaca in their *totoras,* which were 15 feet long and four feet wide and which slid effortlessly between the reeds. This kind of boat still exists today. The *Uros* make them with rushs and bamboo.

Fishing in the Pacific was a little more primitive. Rudimentary boats were used, which the Indians straddled, legs in the water. For open sea fishing, they made rafts or *balsa* with the light, hard wood of the balsa tree and equipped them with a cotton sail. A stone tied to a rope acted as an anchor.

Above, the hunter and the dog, his traditional companion (Mochica culture).

Manufacture and use of boats of plaited rushes, peculiar to Lake Titicaca.

Handing over of the wool for weaving and its uses. Below, present day peasants embroidering.

VIII. CRAFTS

CRAFTSMEN AND THEIR WORK

Crafts were part of the duties or service that the subjects were bound to perform for their master. Thus every family spun and wove for the Inca. The civil servants provided the wool and distributed it, along with cotton and other materials kept in the public storehouses. Once made up, the garments were returned to the storehouses and piled up. As with foodstuffs, the textile stocks were huge and one does not know whether to be surprised or admire the care with which they were treated.

The craftsmen had little imagination, which indicated that the Incas hardly bothered to make use of the heritage left by the Mochicas and Chimus. All the same, great works of art were realized, especially in the field of weaving.

They used bronze scissors and copper hachets skilfully. A simple stone acted as a hammer and a piece of polished flint as a knife. Ropes were made of plaited majagua fibres. Surprisingly, they did not use the wheel. Patience and iron discipline were needed to complete their building projects.

In addition to work done by families, there were of course proper craftsmen—potters, weavers, goldsmiths or sculptors—who were responsible for more elaborate works. Some worked directly for the Court, others were delegated to regional centres, under the direct supervision of the imperial civil servants. These skilled craftsmen were taken away from their community so that they could devote themselves entirely to their art. They were compensated however by being excused all menial tasks. Techniques were generally handed down from father to son.

POTTERY

Mochica pottery covered most subjects, portraying all social levels, representing both the ugly and the beautiful. It gives us the opportunity to make several comparisons between it and the Incas' pottery, which was lighter in colour. A certain number of specimens of Empire pottery have even been preserved—bowls, deep cups, goblets with slightly convex walls and mainly round bottles with a handle covering the top and one or several holes in it.

The potter's wheel was unknown to the Incas and therefore they had to make do with their hands to make dishes and recipients. They sometimes mixed thin corn straw with clay to make it stronger. To make the large jars in which they kept their supplies, they cut clay into long strips and wound it into long cylinders. On the West coast, moulds were used in addition to these two manual and rather primitive techniques, and this made for a kind of series manufacture.

Even if the jars made at the time of the Empire lacked inspiration, they were generally rather delicate, shiny and well-shaped. They were mostly painted in black and white on a red background. They were decorated with geometric designs based on squares, lozenges, triangles and Greek key patterns.

Specimen of Nazca pottery (Lima Museum).

Above, Indian pottery on a terrace in Lima.

The peasants spun the cotton and wool when their housework left them time free. They did it even when they were walking, so long as their hands were not busy with something else.

They used wooden spindles and wound the thread on bamboo sticks or made it into balls. The fibres were coloured with vegetable dyes before being woven. In some regions on the southern coast, the Indians achieved as many as 190 different dyes.

The most common loom, still used today in the Andes, was two sticks to which the threads were attached. One was tied to a tree and the other to the woman's waist.

Below and right, decorative designs of llama wools.

In some regions pottery even had relief or engraved designs, representing scenes from daily, religious or military life or Andean mythology. Some jars or cups even had human or animal shapes on them.

Once decorated, the pieces were oven-baked according to two techniques. In the first, intense heat was used with a powerful draught of air to make them stronger and give them light brown, red or cream tones. In the second, the pots were kept in a cooler oven where there was less oxygen; this made them black and shiny. Pottery then progressed little under the Incas and manufacture was limited to the Cuzco region and those towns run by civil servants.

WEAVING

Women, from peasants to Sun Virgins, were given this particular craft as a responsibility. In the Andes, it was older than pottery. It developed in a spectacular way under the Incas. The raw materials were cotton, grown on the Pacific coast, alpaca and vicuna wool, while llama wool was kept for rougher cloths.

74

There is nothing but admiration to be expressed by the result. During the Incas' time many techniques were practised from the simplest like those used for making ponchos and better quality working clothes, to the most refined. With the latter, gold threads could be mixed with the coloured wool using the makrame method, and for ceremonial cloth, brocading and embroidery were used.

Some pieces of material were over 60 feet long.

Designs were complicated, with only the colour scheme and oblique lines in common. Two-headed men, stylized birds and other mythical creatures were used in polygonal designs. Many of them can still be seen today. Man is always represented with his arms wide open, as if about to seize or embrace.

The designs are repeated in alternation, the subject facing once left, once right, for example. The rich colours already mentioned are of exquisite taste. Complementary colours were often used for the background and the tassels. Ocre went with dark green, purple with golden yellow.

THE ART OF FEATHERS

Although less well developed than by the Aztecs, the art of the feather was not neglected by the Incas.

They mainly used parrot feathers brought from the Amazon forests. Kept in the public storehouses, they were given to the lower classes, whose duty it was to work them.

Feathers were important at ceremonies. There were several kinds of sticks decorated with spreads of three colours (orange, black and yellow), or in blue and red if there were only two. Feathers of all sizes were used, from quills to down. The finest were taken from Sierra humming birds and the craftsmen arranged then without clips or any other kind of device, but with remarkable skill.

Fans were also made to cool the rich and for the headgear that they wore. Although some chiefs wore colourful headgear, rather like Red Indian feathers, the Incas preferred to decorate their llantu with just the odd feather from a bird of prey.

Above, instruments carved from bones (Lima Museum) and a golden necklace (the Cohen collection). Right, a golden necklace of Mochica origin.

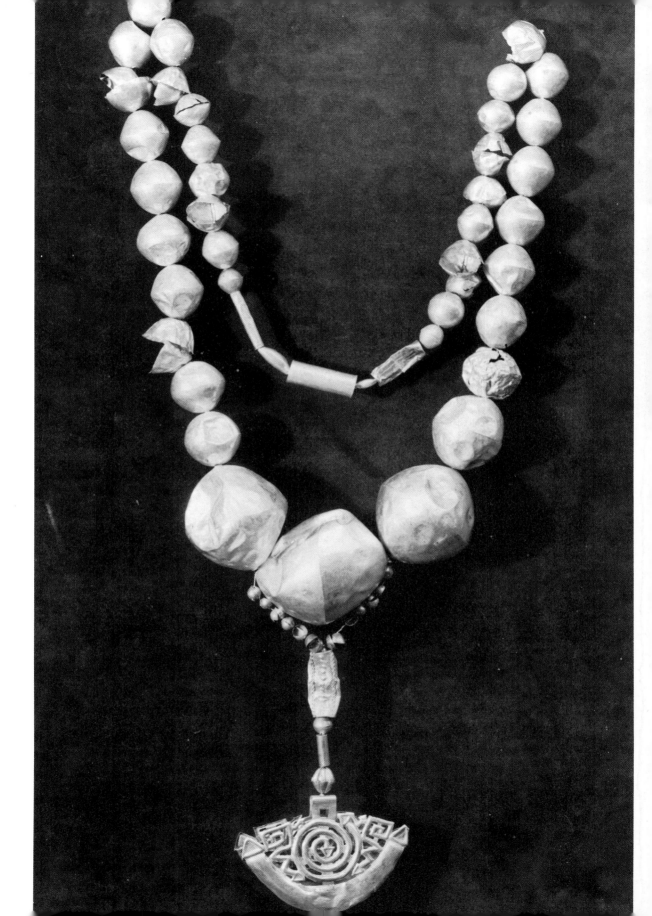

METALS

Iron was unknown to the Incas. They used stone and copper to make their tools, alloying the latter with tin to obtain bronze. However, they acquired expert knowledge of working precious metals such as gold, silver and platinum. The latter was hardly known in Europe and only then after 1730.

Metallurgy was probably born in what now constitutes Colombia. The Chavin civilization already knew how to work gold. Tombs dating from before our era have provided admirable examples. It was however in the Peruvian Andes that metallurgy developed strongest. Nuggets were sifted from river beds and beaten into sheets that could be worked. Gold was also dug from open mines or shallow pits. The Indians dug with picks

made of antlers or with shafts tipped with copper. Once extracted from the seam, the metal was melted in ovens in which holes were made to create draughts. But the Incas never bothered to dig deep for metals.

Metal work was intended for decorative rather than utilitarian purposes. Workshops supplied the large sheets which were intended to cover parts of walls in temples and palaces. Goldsmiths made jewellry that was exclusively reserved for the emperor and important dignataries, such as pendants, bracelets and mainly discs that were fitted to the ears of the mighty. In addition there were many religious objects, among which a kind of crescent-shaped sacrificial knife, so characteristic of the Inca period and called *tumi*.

Although the gold and silver mines belonged exclusively to the Emperor, the *curacas* were responsible for their operation. Control then was local rather than national. The deposits were under constant control, for fear that scraps of the precious metal be stolen.

At their arrival the Spaniards discovered a strange "white gold", alloy of platinum, gold and silver. Made for religious purposes, this metal was reserved for the temple of the Moon, as it was of the same colour. The Spaniards told how they found a sheet more than 25 feet long.

The most important deposit was at Potosi, 15,000 feet high. It was mainly the Spaniards who exploited it, taking over the equipment put in place by the Incas. The miners' work, which was never easy, became a torture after the conquest, and inevitably ended in death.

Opposite, an earring, and, below, an object of worship. Right, a gold funeral mask and a brooch. Below, articles in bronze (that the Incas made by alloying copper and tin).

IX. OTHER TRADES AND PROFESSIONS

THE "MITA", A KIND OF FORCED DUTY

The Andean population spent most of its time on agricultural work. However, it was forced to fulfil certain duties such as leaving home to take part in the great collective work projects for the good of the State.

The *mita* was a kind of obligatory duty, like those known in Europe during the Middle Ages. Civil servants recruited the Indians in rotation following strict methods and the needs of the moment. Only men were taken.

Called by royal order the peasant left his *ayllu*. The State looked after him, while the community to which he belonged looked after his fields, thus replying to the principle of solidarity. This system allowed the State to have a large army at disposal and also to build realizations necessary to its prosperity, such as roads, bridges, public buildings and to mine minerals.

At the beginning of the Empire, all those called for the *mita* could be used for any of the different tasks. Later, however, some regions trained their men for special duties, to prepare them for a specific job, which was then passed down from father to son. Some parts specialized in woodwork, some trained miners, others builders or stone masons.

As the relay was always on hand, the duration of the *mita* was the same for everybody. Once this period was finished, the Indian went back to his village, reintegrated his community, and carried on his agricultural work, until he was called up again.

MILITARY SERVICE

So that the men would not lose all the benefits of military training, they were made to carry out exercises and manoeuvres several times a month, after they had got back to the village.

The Indians fought with bows and arrows, spears, sabres and little star-shaped stone clubs. They protected their heads with rather rudimentary wooden helmets, while the nobles and chiefs covered theirs with ornaments. Each company flew its flag next to the royal standard, which was decorated with a rainbow, the emblem of the Empire.

The soldiers had to do long forced marches. They mostly spent the night in storehouses, where there was food and arms. Although women were less directly concerned with war, they sometimes accompanied their husbands, carrying their packs and making their meals.

The army crossed inhabited regions in perfect order, without causing the slightest damage to the peasants. Disobedience and disorder were severely punished. Lack of respect to private property, for example, was punished by death.

In wartime, the troops went to the front. The

The vase shown on the left-hand page shows a blind man holding a begging cup. Below, a scraper.

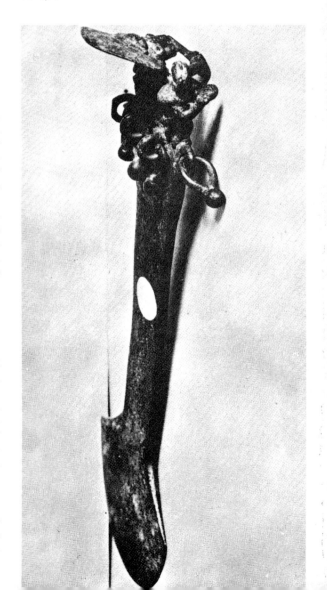

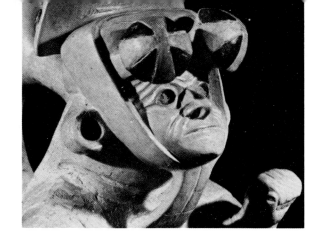

Inca personally directed operations. He was extremely prudent, far preferring negotiations to direct attack. His hope was that the enemy would simply surrender, psychologically crushed as it was by the powerful army drawn up before it. Violence was avoided, though without neglecting anything that might encourage surrender, such as destroying crops, and propaganda. If peace propsoals came of this, the Inca took the opportunity to subdue yet another region without bloodshed. If, on the other hand, the enemy was determined and brave, the Inca attacked without further ceremony, cutting off the heads of all those who resisted him.

The Inca looked after his men wisely and with method. It was important that they be strong, as his power finally depended on them.

If the climate did not suit those come from another region for a particular battle, he replaced them with fit men, sending the weak back home to be looked after.

Contrary to the Aztecs, the Incas tried to occupy conquered regions without paralysing daily life or work. They took over slowly, little by little obtaining cooperation from their new subjects, progressively making them comply with their laws and with Sun worship.

The vases show Inca warriors.

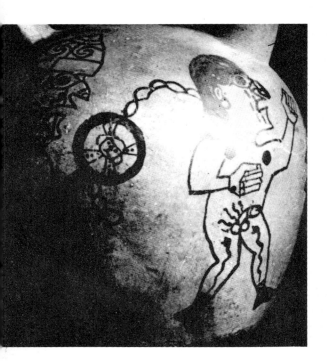

SERVING THE INCA

There were many people in the Inca's service and that of his relations, making life agreeable, looking after the needs of all the inhabitants of the palace, who included the sons of chiefs who lived in Cuzco for their studies. Apart from domestics, such as cooks and chambermaids, there were guards responsible for protecting the palace walls and the storehouses, and inspectors, whose job it was to manage weaving and the making of royal garments. Then there were deliverymen who supplied the Court, gardeners, market-gardeners, architects, responsible for making models for new building projects, as well as sweepers, water-carriers, litter bearers for the royal palanquin, etc. It seems there was even a sort of clown called *canichu* in Quechua, who, of course, was supposed to make everybody laugh.

All these jobs, even the meanest, were coveted by the people, as they were a way to direct contact with the sovereign, and provided the great honour of looking after his home and even his person. A good servant was rewarded when he became old or passed on his job to another member of the family, to the one who seemed the most suitable and most faultless, combining faithfulness and skill. When he took over a job, the servant was playing with the fate of his whole *ayllu*. Any mistake he made could have disastrous consequences for the community.

84

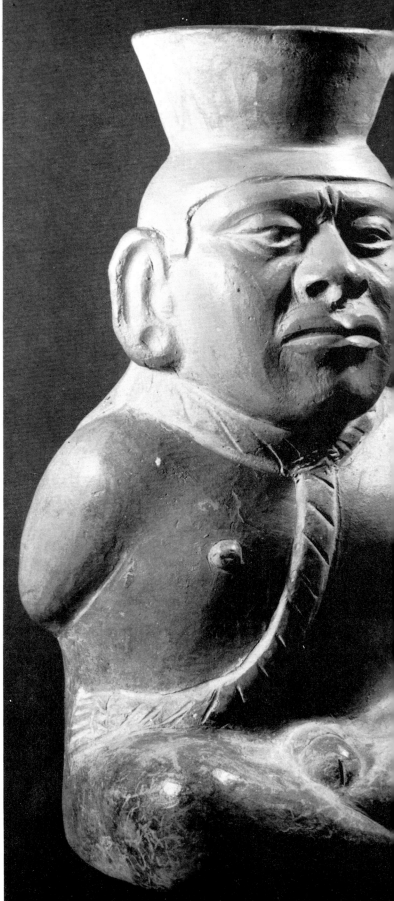

Far left, a warrior holding a prisoner. Opposite, a jar also showing a prisoner (the Cummings Collection, Chicago). Right, a Mochica golden mask.

THE YANAS, WEALTHY SLAVES

The was no slavery as such in the Empire. There were, however, a number of Indians called *yanas,* who, in certain respects, could be called "serfs" or simply "eternal servants". Their origins went back to a revolt which resulted in several thousands of Indians being deported to the town of *Yanacu,* where they were to have been executed. But the empress reigning at the time intervened and their sentence was changed to perpetual slavery for them as well as their descendants. The *yanas* were not counted in censuses to deny them all right to existence.

They were mainly placed in the Inca's service. Some were assigned to farming the royal lands, and others to the temples and palace.

As valets and bodyguards for the Emperor and his chiefs they learnt how to win their trust and esteem. Thus, when the Emperor made a exceptional present to one of his civil servants, he often gave one or several *yanas.* The *yana's* job was handed down from the father to one of the sons. The others went back to their village of origin where they became full citizens.

Because of their faithfulness, *yanas* were given increasingly important jobs, and although clothed and fed by their masters there were little by little allowed possessions such as houses, land or herds. The richest among them were offered noblemen's daughters in marriage, which opened the doors of the aristocracy to them. It was thus that some of the humblest among them became powerful across the generations and this is why it is difficult to be sure what the real position of the *yanas* was, that of slaves or upstarts.

THE INSPECTORS OF THE EMPIRE

A well-oiled control system was needed to ensure the smooth running of this eminently centralized machine that was the Empire. The Incan administrative apparatus was based on immobilism and a foolproof organization.

The emperor put only a limited trusted in his provincial governors. This is why he had the entire population controlled in a spread across the four quarters of the Empire. In addition to the strict hierarchy of civil servants responsible for applying the laws of the kingdom, there were those known as the inspectors. Their Quechua name *tokoyrikok* means "he to whom nothing escapes". They belonged to the imperial caste and received an insignia from the emperor himself which was the proof of the official nature of their mission.

However, they went around incognito, so that they could make spot checks on life, anywhere, at any time, on tax payment or make inventories of soldiers personal effects or count the available workers.

These inspectors, as direct representatives of the emperor, were given free board and lodgings by the authorities of the towns or villages they visited. They checked up on everything, from the *curacas'* activities to the Indians' meals (which is why the curtain which acted as a door to the Indian's hut had to be left open while they ate). They carried out interrogations and gathered data on offences and crimes to report directly to the emperor.

If he found it necessary, the Inca delegated special judges to travel to the place of crime, and, if the case was very serious, he went there himself to apply the law and respect justice. He was all-powerful, and civil servants, chiefs and peasants were equal in their powerlessness.

In addition, the data communicated by the inspectors gave the Inca the opportunity to carefully prepare his annual meeting with governors and civil servants when they came to present the accounts of their districts.

X. ROUTES OF COMMUNICATION

ROADS

The Inca civilization, with its idea of order and rationalization, set up a road network that elicited the Spaniards' admiration during the conquest. Overcoming the numerous topographical difficulties of the Andes, they traced out communication routes which can be easily compared with those built by the Romans.

The geography of the Empire was essentially split into two totally distinct zones: the flat and arid coastal strip, and the Cordillera. The Incas built two important roads running from north to south, in each of these zones. The Spaniards named them Plains highway (camino de los Llanos) and Mountain highway (camino de la Sierra).

Naturally, the building of this second road presented enormous problems. The Incas, however, were equal to them. Their idea was to make roads as straight as possible, changing them into stair-

ways where the incline was steep. Elsewhere, they followed the more gentle slopes or went through tunnels, which reached lengths of 15 feet and which were dug in natural depressions.

The roads were cobbled or paved. Uneven ground was levelled with a mixture called *pirca* and which consisted of clay, pebbles and crushed corn leaves. It was firm enough to provide good resistance to all weathers. If a road ran through fields, these were marked off with boundary posts. Stones were also used to mark the edge of pathways where there was a risk of sand being blown over them.

The Indians even made supporting walls at each side of a road, planted trees, and dug ditches. There were signposts everywhere. Width varied, reaching 15 feet in the plains, while, on the Andean slopes, it narrowed to three feet.

The upkeep of routes of communication was the responsibility of the inhabitants of the regions

The remains of the gate shown on the left were found in Colombia. Below, a vase with four figures, two of whom are carrying a hammock in which is a nobleman; the fourth is holding the edge of the hammock to control its movement (Musée de l'Homme, Paris).

that they crossed. The main user was the Inca with his *chasquis* and soldiers. As we have already seen, the Indians travelled rarely, except to go to market.

THE TWO MAIN ROUTES

The coastal road started in the Gulf of Guayaquil, which is now in Ecuador, crossing the ancient kingdom of Chimu and arriving at the place where Lima stands today; at the time, it was only a little village. It continued south, crossing great sandy zones, as well as the Ica and Nazca valleys, carrying on through a desolate landscape as far as the Atacama desert, near the present capital of Chile. This was the limit of the Empire.

The Sierra road began on the banks of the Rio Auscamayo, which now acts as a border between Columbia and Ecuador, crossed Quito, climbing through valleys and over passes with the snow-covered peaks for a background. It linked the major towns, such as Cajamarca, Jauja and the capital, Cuzco, continued south, skirting Lake Titicaca and the ruins of Tihuanaco before passing via Cochabamba, Sucre and the famous mines of Potosi. It ended after more than 3,000 miles in the Tucuman region, which today belongs to Argentina.

A network of secondary roads, which followed valleys and passes, joined the two main roads at several points. A *tambo,* a sort of inn, was placed about every 15 miles, providing bed and board for the traveller. It had a common dormitory for peasants and soldiers, and even a few rooms for travelling personalities, a llama enclosure, and a storehouse where the guests' food was kept.

BRIDGES

There were obviously terrible difficulties in building mountain roads. There were fast-swelling rivers and deep gorges to be crossed. The building of the famous suspension bridges demanded all the skill of the Inca engineers.

These bridges were hung by four cables "the thickness of a man's thigh", and made of extremely strong majagua fibres. It required a tremendous effort to pass the cables from one side to another and tie them to a boulder or column of stone. They were linked by thinner ropes along the whole length of the bridge to make the deck. Sometimes ramps were made. With or without a hand-rail, the bridges

88

Opposite, two people on a road at the time of the Incas. Note the small buildings which were postal relays.

impressed the Spaniards, although some would only cross them, as they revealed later, on all fours.

In fact they were remarkably solid. Keepers tended them all the time and kept them in working condition. For this they charged a toll, which was payed in cash.

Moreover, the bridges were rebuilt every two years. In case of war or invasion, they were burnt, to cut the enemy's route.

There were also wooden footbridges, of a type that is still common, for crossing smaller rivers, and also the *croja*, a more picturesque way of crossing powerful torrents. The traveller was hung in a basket tied to a tree trunk, which in turn was hung from a cable on which he slid from one bank to the other. The attendant on the opposite side pulled a rope to move the basket down the natural bend in the cable. The first part was easy as the basket went downwards, but then it became more difficult. Sometimes, the rope which the attendant pulled with all his might, snapped. The luckless traveller was then stuck while repairs were carried out. He tried to keep his cool as best he could, while only inches from the water, or actually in it.

The *tarabita* was even more primitive. It consisted in crossing a river hanging onto a rope, using hands and legs like a gymnast. In the coastal zone, the waters ran more slowly and the banks were more accessible. Rivers were crossed on rafts tied to a cable and poles were used to propel the craft.

Left and above, suspension bridges.

THE MAIL

The Inca Yuaupangui is generally supposed to have set up the postal service.

The postmen, or *chasquis,* worked only for the State. To be a messenger, one had to be fast and well trained. One trained for the job from childhood. The *chasquis* wore a uniform and were easily recognized by their feathered hat, star-shaped frond and conch which they used to announce their arrival. They worked in twos, fours or sixes—depending on the amount of mail there was to carry—

in cabins which stood at the roadside at varying distances from one another, though near enough to allow the postman to complete his journey between them without slowing his rhythm. They were built on open ground, and two *chasquis* watched the road in each direction. As soon as one saw a dispatch rider, he went out to meet him and ran alongside him to pick up the message without slowing or stopping. The message might be verbal or in the shape of a packet or *quipu.* The *chasqui* who took the relay went off at full speed, while the other stopped to rest and eat before setting off again. In this way, up to 200 miles a

day could be covered.

The postmen, who were sworn to secrecy, were of never-failing trustworthiness. However, it was probable that the most important messages were sent in code. But it was thanks to the *chasquis* that the Emperor had fresh fish on his table every day, caught in the sea or Lake Titicaca, as well as tropical fruit. If the delivery was of special im-portance or was adressed directly to the emperor, the *chasqui* carried a red sash or a stick covered with notches. If there was a revolt or an invasion, the messengers lit fires at the door of their cabin to give the alert.

The postal service provided the Incas with an efficient and speedy control over all that went on in the Empire.

Left, a Mochica mask. Above a chasqui's (postman) horn. Below, a present day market in Cuzco, just like in ancient times.

XI. BUSINESS

THE LOVE OF STATISTICS

The Incas made wide use of statistics, which were also an excellent instrument of control. They numbered, counted, catalogued. Nothing escaped their attention, either on a national scale, or on a local scale. A chronicler tells how difficult, even impossible, it was to hide a simple pair of sandals.

It should not be forgotten that the Incas did not know how to write and had no developed monetary system. How then did they take a census of the population, record production, count herds and all other factors which made up the administration of a centralized state?

In ancient Peru, as in the West, the decimal system was used and goods (precious metals and medicinal herbs most of all) were weighed on single or double scales. With these two discoveries and using great ingenuity, ambitious projects were realized. Operations were carried out using a sort of abacus, shown in Poma de Aayala's drawings (which were at the same time naive and instructive). This mathematical instrument consisted of five rows in which one to five corn seeds were put. Results were noted on the *quipu*, a remarkable invention of the period.

THE QUIPU

The *quipu* was to the Incas what computers are to us. It consisted first of all of a grey-white cord, which could be from a few inches or three feet long. It was held horizontally. From it hung 48 strings divided into 5 groups, with extra threads added. Altogether there could be up to 87 laces that were knotted starting at the bottom, the first series corresponding to units, the second to tens, etc. The largest number that could be used was 100,000. The strings were of different colours, each corresponding to different objects or people. The knots, which were of varying sizes and spacings, marked the numbers, zero being represented by the absence of a knot in a given section. Black meant the weather; red, the army; green, the enemy; yellow, gold; and white, silver.

Left above, a quipu and how to use it. Below, a photo taken in Cuzco, showing the pottery merket.

The strings also indicated hierarchies. When an inventory of weapons was being made, for example, the first strings were kept for spears, the nobleman's arm. They were followed by javelins, arrows and catapults, in that order of importance. As regards demography, men came first, by order of age, then women and children.

Many *quipus*, held by the central administration, alone contained the whole life of the Empire in numbers.

The operation and understanding of *quipus* was the sole task of experts named *quipucamayos* or "quipu keepers". The handling of the strings demanded a perfectly trained memory and was also handed down from father to son. Each *quipucamayo* was specialized in a particular field. Some recorded warehoused goods, others registered births, deaths and marriages, others counted the men available for war. Mistakes had to be avoided at all costs; any omission or error was punished by death. Less qualified accountants were used to take note of all community activities. They kept the *quipucamayos* up to date for them to group data on several simple *quipus*. The collected data added to a total which was communicated to the emperor.

This ingenious mnemo-technical system had one shortcoming, however: it was not standardized. Thus one *quipucamayo* was not able to interpret *quipus* belonging to other colleagues. It took archeologists a long time to discover this.

TRADE

Not surprisingly trade was centralized and was mainly done by barter between civil servants, communities and even regions. Products and artefacts from the coast were exchanged against those of the sierra, and there was a better system of distribution than in a more regionalized society.

Trade between individuals or neighbouring communities was carried out in all simplicity and bore more psychological than economic importance. To the Indian used to a life that was as organized as it was monotonous, going to a neighbouring market was a cause for rejoicing. The fun he got from it was his main profit. Goods were rare and not very valuable.

There were only leftovers, as nearly everything disappeared into the state storehouses. The leftovers could be interesting if the crop was good; there was also a tiny selection of handicrafts, made in rare moments of freedom.

Markets were held three times a month in the bigger towns and the better part of the population of nearby villages attended. What might be termed export trade went on in the border regions or with isolated, newly-conquered communities.

In principle, newly-annexed provinces had a status of semi-liberty while the laws and standards of the Empire were being instituted. As long as the administrative machine was not installed, soldiers and inhabitants of border regions traded happily, exchanging as many products as possible. The all-powerful Inca left them alone to gain his advantage from it. He was the first to taste new produce and also benefitted from information that traders brought back. In fact, these people were also spies, as in the Aztec civilization.

STRANGELY SILENT MARKETS

Market days were therefore something of a holiday. On the eve of the *catu,* and with due permission from the chief, man and wife set out accompanied by other villagers and carrying produce and *chicha* as well as products for barter.

The journey was often long and tiring, but nothing could dampen the enthusiasm of going to the marketplace. The peasants spent the night by the roadside curled up in a ball.

Left, a chief counting the amount of seed provided by the peasants on a quipu. Below, market scene.

In addition to exchanges that could be made, the market was also a place where they could dance in groups, listen to storytellers, and, of course, drink as much as they liked.

The wife looked after the real trading. Sitting or squatting on the ground with her heaps of flour, spice or wheat before her, she stayed motionless for hours waiting for a customer, watching the pageant of colours and faces that paraded before her.

The men looked after the buying, first going around the market, slowly and attentively, and strangely enough, in silence. But everyone was quite happy. Only the sound of clothes rubbing together, footsteps, and the noise of the gestures that accompanied the negotiations were to be heard, mingled with the muffled sound of flutes and tambourines from the nearby streets.

When a peasant found an interesting bargain, he squatted opposite the Indian woman and took from his bag the article he was willing to barter. If the peasant woman was not happy with the offer she remained impassive, eyes gazing into space. The man then added more goods, until the women's interest was aroused. She quickly grabbed what was offered and the man took his share. The whole deal took place without a word being exchanged, not even an "hello".

Once the bargaining was over, the Indian woman went back to her dreaming. The peasant, for his part, went shuffling off to the dancers to drink *chicha*.

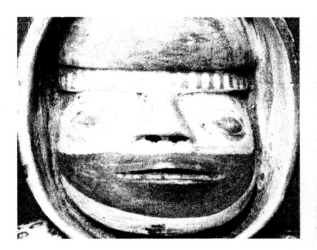

XII. PASTIMES

THE ANDEAN TEMPERAMENT

The Indian of the high plateau combined two frames of mind, which at first might seem contradictory, but which in fact were complementary. The first aspect of his personality was that of reserve, even melancholy.

His life was overshadowed by his work, which he did methodically and submissively, without speaking economy of mouvement. The second side to him was joyful, even exuberant, and showed at games and on holidays.

Once on holiday, the Indian spent his energy without thinking, loved exaggeration both in singing, dancing, stories and the way of telling them. He liked sarcasm and irony. Stories were accompanied by mighty bursts of laughter and exclamations. His favourite expression was "gua". But, according to the Spanish chroniclers, he expressed himself best with eyes and hands.

Workdays were so filled that there was hardly any time for games. Festivities, however, gave the people the opportunity of letting their hair down. Markets were not the only opportunity for amusement. According to historians, there were about 100 holidays, at which not everybody could take part, obviously. It was then that meals were eaten in common and everybody brought his share. These more or less modest feasts were the occasion for drinking, singing and dancing.

GAMES

Games of chance were very popular among the Incas and their subjects, despite the strict organization of their society, or perhaps because of it. The conquerors themselves became passion-

Left: vase decoration originating from the south coast and deliberately funny. Below, a procession.

ately fond of them too. The most popular was dice, which was played mostly at banquets. The Indians, squatting or standing, formed little circles and the games were accompanied by shouts and exclamations. The dice were in wood or bone and the sides numbered 1, 2, 3, 4, 5 and 20 respectively.

They were used for playing *wayru*, a kind of game of goose. Pebbles or dried beans acted as pawns. The game's name apparently comes from the name of one of the concubines of the Inca Tupac Yuapanqui. The emperor won a game hands down in this young lady's presence. Believing that she brought him luck, he made her a present of the jewel he had won and commanded that the game should bear her name.

Chuncara was played with seeds of different colours. They were put onto a slate of stone with five holes in it, each worth 10, 20, 30, 40 and 50 points. The first to get the highest number won.

The Incas loved *apaytalla*, invented apparently by the wife of the great Pachacuti to amuse the imperial entourage. It was a game of skill, consisting simply of making a seed jump as far as possible from its pod by pressing it between two fingers. The noise made by the seed when it fell was also important in deciding the winner.

Some games were of a ritual nature. Dice was played at burials and it was supposed to be death itself which decided the winner.

If it can be called a game, then the practice of whipping the legs with bindings or ropes, which was linked to magic, should be mentioned. The Indians often beat themselves, not only as a sign of penitence, but also to stimulate themselves, test their respective endurance or simply for pleasure.

Sporting competitions were almost exclusively reserved for members of the aristocracy. Those entered by the sons of *curacas* and young noblemen, before becoming *orejones* have already been mentioned. They took place on the main squares of towns, often surrounded by grandstands (as at Machu Picchu). Whilst in their seats, people took the opportunity of bartering the odd piece of merchandise.

The child's favourite toy was the top. It is surprising to note that this game is common to practically all primitive civilizations. Girls had no dolls, as they were used as charms and accompanied the dead to the grave.

XIII. DANCING AND MUSIC

AT COURT

Dancing is an element of expression in all civilizations. On the high plateau, it revealed the joy, yearnings and mystique of the Andean peasant. The Quechua word *taqui* covers all beats, melodies and rhythms that were at the base of Inca music.

The inhabitants of the Empire were born dancers, at all levels of society. However, distinction must be made between popular dancing and the more solemn dancing of the nobility, which had an essentially religious character to it. The people mixed religion and profane, and even orgy. While dancing, the peasants often drank quantities of *chicha* to bring about a state of trance.

On the main square of Cuzco, members of the Court performed the *way-yaya*. Men and women separated to form two ranks, which went hand in hand, slowly and with dignity towards the Inca. To the beat of of a large drum, hung from a man's back and played by a woman, they took two steps forward and one back.

The snake dance had more or less the same steps, except that the dancers carried a multi-coloured rope with the head of a snake at one end. Under the gaze of the Inca and the empty stare of the mummies brought out from the Sun temple or their once palace for the occasion, the rhythmic movements of the dancers made the "body" move. The *orejones* and their wives also danced to a more gay rhythm, in little groups of three. The man held the hands of two women who spun round on the spot.

POPULAR DANCES

As already seen, the energetic, tumultuous style of popular dances contrasted with the more static style of ritual Court relaxations. Both men and women took part in a joyful, lively explosion. War dances, which took place after the battle, expressed the joy of victory with great leaps and shouts.

Popular dances repeated the acts of daily life, the moments of joy and sadness, of hope and work with movements that were sometimes near to pantomime. Cheerfulness dominated all of

Left and right, musicians with various instruments.

them, be it the shepherd's or *llamaya* dance, the *harahuayo* or farmer's dance, the *cachihua* or dance of joy, or the *haylli arahui*—the dance of victory. Their theatrical aspect was enhanced by costumes sometimes made of animal skins decorated with little bells, and even by the use of tools, whose symbolism was evident.

Among these popular dances—many of which still exist today in the Andes—some were less lively. There was the slow step of the llama shepherds dance that the Indians performed to the soft sounds of the flute and among beasts decorated with little bells and covered with cloth made of their own wool.

Puli-puli dancers covered their bodies with feathers while *pariane* dancers dressed as birds to implore the water god. In the *chaco*, the dancers surrounded the musicians in a large circle. The women carried sticks while the men were armed with catapults. These was even a potato dance, in which the Indian women shook a blanket while making the gesture of throwing seeds to the wind.

Festival scenes after Ayala.

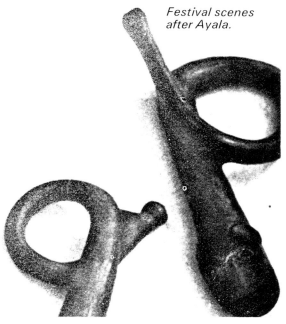

100

The idea behind the *huaillia,* one of the best know dances, was the same. Peasants beat the earth with rapid little steps in order to encourage the soil to become more fertile.

INSTRUMENTS

Andean music was passed down from generation to generation, evolving all the time. The instruments were mainly wind and percussion, as strings were unknown in Peru until the 16th century.

Among the wind instruments, the most remarkable were without doubt flutes. The *quena* should be mentioned first as it was the most traditional. Made of bone or bamboo, it was in fact a simple recorder with a minor scale of five notes from so to la, missing out fa. Essentially a shepherd's instrument, it added a nostalgic sound to the magical landscape of the Andes. To give it heavy and disquieting resonances, the Indians, who occasionally indulged in mysticism, blew it into a

101

clay bowl. The *quena* perfectly expressed the deep inherent melancholy in the Indian temperament.

The *zampona,* or Pan's flute, was generally made of bamboo, sometimes of wood, earth or metal, and was laid out in two rows of tubes that were graduated in length. It is still well known today. The shepherds improvised in groups on their *zamponas* and *quenas,* playing in perfect harmony.

As we have seen, the *chasquis* used a conch called the *puturutu* to announce their arrival at postal relays. There were also terra cotta or wooden trumpets, the ocarina and a little flute called the *pincullu,* which was carved from lama bones.

Percussion instruments were extremely varied, with drums and tambourines of all kinds, gourds, bells and finally a kind of sleigh-bell which was tied around the ankles.

MUSICOS E INSTRUMENTOS

XIV. LEGAL ORGANIZATION AND TAXES

JUSTICE AND MORALS

The Inca was only able to guarantee the proper working of his complex administrative organ by instituting laws of a severity that was striking. It is clear, however, that an infraction of the law such as leaving a place of work (the guarding of a bridge, for instance), an error on a *quipu* or an order incompletely carried out, could have consequences that could affect a community, an army or the supply of a region. The emperor Pachacuti is credited with a whole series of maxims defining the morals used in the Empire. It is difficult to establish to what point oral tradition and the writings of chroniclers modified them. Nevertheless, they provide us with the portrait of an emperor who was mostly known for his wisdom and integrity.

Several of these maxims concern desire and the unhappiness that this brings, for example: "Jealousy is a worm which eats the entrails of the envious". Others speak of anger, drunkenness, and madness or recommend the punishments that thieves, adulterers and murderers deserve. Advice and rules of conduct were unsparingly lavished on those who held governors' posts, and to healers and accountants. There is another maxim which seems to moderate the above and probably sums up the essence of Inca moral in the field of rights: "If justice is to prevail, then it should be done with care".

This is why there was a certain flexibility: theft, for example, was punished differently if it was committed for greed and desire for possesion or if it was simply due to hunger. In the latter case, the civil servant in charge of food distribution was taken to task. It was his responsibility to avoid underfeeding. The defendant's age was also taken into account. Habitual criminals were punished more severely than others.

In addition, the legal system was not standardized. Provinces and even regions maintained their traditions. Everything concerning community life was generally judged clemently. However, it was not the same for crimes against the Empire's organization or the sovereign's person. Any rebellion or attempt at rebellion was harshly stamped out, even suspicion could bring the death penalty, as could refusal to pay taxes, fraud or premeditated crime.

JUDGES AND TRIALS

Justice was not put into the hands of specialists. For community problems, it was obviously chiefs who looked after it, acting as justices of the peace, arbitrating conflicts, organizing the distribution of water for spraying the fields, fencing fields, and keeping harmony in the *ayllu*. More serious offences were looked after by the *curacas* and civil servants. The inspectors, who roamed the Empire to carry out controls, were also made responible for inquests and particularly delicate procedures. They sent their results to a 12-man tribunal specially set up by the Inca. The emperor went in person to judge *orejones* and important dignataries and was assisted by four counsellors.

Trials never lasted more than two or three days. The judge in charge summoned the accused as well as all those who were in any way connected with the affair in hand. They were called to make a declaration, after which evidence was examined. The judge then passed sentence. Sometimes torture was used to obtain confessions or soothsayers were consulted and invited to give their opinion on the case. There was no right of appeal.

Once the verdict was passed, the judge informed his immediate superior who, in turn, passed on information concerning the affair to the upper levels of the administrative hierarchy, until it finally came to the Inca. Prisons were mainly preventive. Prisoners from the privileged classes received favourable treatment. In fact they continued to be served by their domestics and were regularly visited.

Chroniclers also speak of a cell full of wild beasts, snakes and toads in which an ordeal took place. The defendant was locked up in it for 48 hours and his survival was proof of his innocence.

PUNISHMENTS AND SENTENCES

Punishments meted out at trials varied a lot. Mostly they were corporal. In his Chronicle,

The engraving opposite shows a man and a woman hung by their hair for adultery.

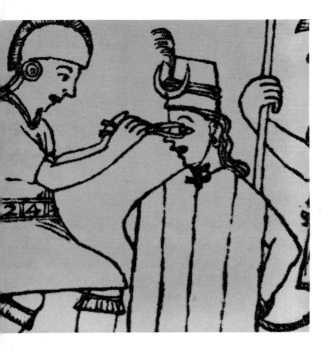

Poma de Ayala gives an impressive list of them. It seems that in principle, the lower classes were more severely punished than the nobility or members of the administrative classes.

Members of the aristocracy could be beheaded or were given a life sentence. Their property was seized or they were simply given a public ordeal: an admonishment or head shaving. One harsh punishment that the rich were also liable to was loss of an eye.

Traitors were stoned, adulterous couples were hung by the hair until they died; those who dared to seduce a "Sun Virgin" were hung by their feet to die slowly.

The lower classes were punished in a less subtle way. They were stoned or hung, the bodies of bad criminals were in addition burned. The whip

was the most common punishment, with a specific number of strokes laid down in the sentence. Some judges deported peasants to the unhealthy coca plantations in the jungle. Floggings were also prescribed.

The Indian then had a vested interest in keeping to his duties and resisting the temptation of breaking the monotonous daily routine. If he obeyed then he would lead a life of dignity with responsibilities sometimes giving way to moments of relaxation, It needed the arrival of the Spaniards to upset this balance.

Mancio Sierra de Lequizamo, one of the Spanish missionaries accompanying Pizarro, sent a long confession to his king before dying, denouncing the excesses committed during the conquest, Among other things, he wrote to the sovereign that "We found lands where there were no thieves nor idle, no vice nor adultery. People did honest and useful jobs." Further, condemning the Spaniards' guilt, he said: "We have changed the Indians entirely, sowing disorder as we went. This country has gone from one extreme to another. It seems that at one time evil did not exist, today it is good which seems to have disappeared."

TAXES

The tribute-money that the Indians paid the Inca was not a fixed sum. It changed according to the needs of the Empire and the age of its subjects. Thus, work accomplished during a lifetime and services rendered (military service, mining, etc.) often constituted the main tax.

We have already mentioned the *mita,* and we also know that the peasants grew, spun, weaved and made clothes for the emperor. We have already told how the State rewarded these efforts by providing for each citizen. Some writers speak of the frugality of the peasant's existence, others, William Prescott, for instance, claim that it would have been difficult to improve on the system of distribution and that the government never lost sight of the well-being of its workers. One thing is sure: even for the hardest jobs, the Indian's health was looked after.

In addition to work, a material contribution was demanded of everyone, however modest. Thus, the poorest populations, such as those from the very North of the Empire, sent bags of fleas as tributes to the emperor, as proof of their fidelity and cleanliness!

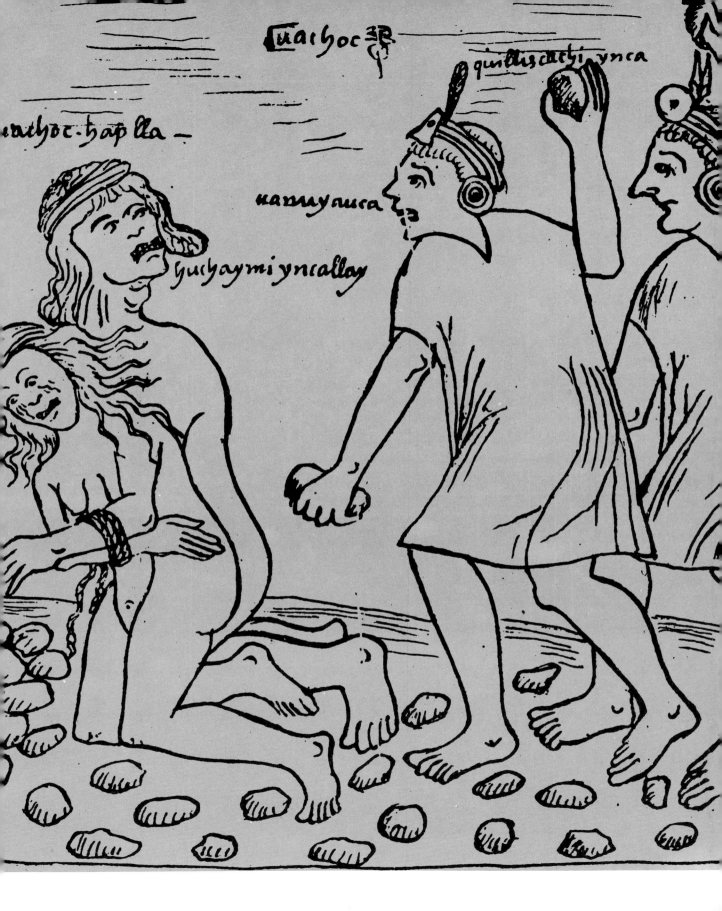

XV. MEDICINE

HEALERS AND SURGEONS

In developing the sciences, the Incas laid special stress on medicine. In fact it was closely linked to magic.

Healers had marvellous knowledge of the properties of plants and minerals. They mostly belonged to the *Colahuaya* tribe, related to the *Uros* and resident not far from Lake Titicaca. Living for part of the year as nomads, they went through towns and villages offering their services. The *Colahuayas'* reputatation in fact still exists today. They continue to scour the high plateau, offering herbs and potions in markets and villages. Their heartiness is famous.

Those inhabitants of the Empire who were not fit for heavy duties—the physically handicapped, mutilated, hunchbacks, etc—were put on research work on medicinal plants and observation of their curative virtues.

Surgeons were remarkably skilled. They carried out amputations, removed tumors, opened abcesses and ulcers and even performed trepannings. Skulls found at excavations have proved this. A skull showing five successive trepannings has even been found. It certainly belonged to the skeleton of a soldier, as surgeons were in great demand after battles, and one of their leading jobs was to repair heads broken by blows from maces or clubs.

ILLNESSES

The most common illnesses were bronchitis and pneumonia, mostly caused by the harshness of the climate and insufficient clothing. The Indians also suffered from warts and a type of leprosy, known as *uta*. The warts, which from time to time broke out all over the skin of both the Indians and even their beasts, could bring on high fever and bleeding. *Uta* especially affected the face. Surgeons used the knife to get rid of it, cutting off the affected parts; some *Chimu* painted vases and bas-reliefs show these mutilations.

Another common sickness was shock or *susto*,

Doctors went from city to city offering their services. Left, a practician at work.

as the Spaniards called it. It could be brought on by a gust of wind, the sight of blood, draughts or even spirits called up by witch doctors. Rheumatism, colic, and tonsilitis were also common. On the other hand, scarlet fever and measles were unknown, although the Indians were to get to know them after the conquest, and many lives were lost to them.

MEDICINES

The Incas used every remedy that nature provided. They treated themselves by fasting, purges, massages, bleedings and with medicinal herbs. They healed wounds with the sap of *molle*, a shrub of the pepper plant family and fought fever with the leaves of yellow-flowered chicory, bark and cactus sap. There were several ways of preparing purges. For example, decoctions of roots or envelopes of corn ears were made. Plants such as *quinaquina* had multiple uses. Scrapings of its wood cleared the liver, its juice had healing virtues, its roast seeds gave off vapours which calmed headaches.

Other herbs are still in use, such as *yuca* leaves, which, when cooked, calm rheumatic pains, or *quinua*, which is beneficial for throat infections. These are just a few examples from a list that could be a lot longer.

Among the minerals, edible clay should be mentioned; it relieved gout; and crushed jasper, used to stop bleeding. In addition, some animals were supposed to have specific properties. The viper bite, for instance, was said to cure certain nervous diseases as well as impotence; bee stings were claimed to relieve rheumatism and ants were supposed to attenuate mental deficiency. Even human excrement had a part to play. The nauseating smell chased away bad spirits. Urine was mainly used because of its amoniac content. Each family kept a small reserve. It was heated and used to rub the temples of those suffering from migraine. It was even used to rub gums and throat. Children who had a temperature were rubbed with it.

Some cures were more of a charm than medicine: potatoes which rheumatics put on the painful parts of their body, for instance. This old woman's cure has travelled and can still be found in many places even today.

COCA

It is impossible to speak of Inca medicine without mentioning *coca*, called *cuca* by the Indians. This five-foot high bush grows in wet regions, mainly in the tropical zones, and its leaves were picked three times a year and dried in the sun. Before taking it, it was mixed with *quinua* ashes and lemon juice. Taken in small doses, the alkaloids in this plant act as a stimulant and provide enormous resistance to hunger and fatigue.

Coca was also used for pharmaceutical purposes. It stopped haemorrhage and vomiting. Taken as a drink, it fought diarrhea and colic, and its juice was used to dry ulcers and wounds. Surgeons gave their patients a combination of these two elements as an anesthetic. In addition coca was also used in certain religious ceremonies. Its leaves were offered to the huacas and the Sun god. Priests ate it during certain rites.

However, coca production was limited, because only members of the nobility and the clergy had the right to use it for other things than medicine and peasants could only use it with special permission.

The Spaniards upset these customs. As soon as they saw the advantage they could take from these narcotic leaves, they increased the number of plantations and permitted their consumption. This allowed them to increase work rate while feeding the Indians less. In the fields and mines, coca was the Indian's only support.

MAGIC AND THE "SITOWA" CEREMONY

Medicine went hand in hand with a certain number of religious and magic rites. The sick person used offerings and sacrifices as much as medicine to ward off evil spirits. If his efforts seemed insufficient, then the witchdoctor was called in.

His first job was to find the origin of the sickness. He rubbed the patient's skin with a cloth or fur, which be then threw away, or he sucked the infected part. The witchdoctor claimed to be immune to sickness thanks to the exorcisms he proclaimed and mostly to the large quantities of coca and *chicha* that he had the right to take.

A purification ceremony called *sitowa* took place every September in Cuzco, and, to the

The ancient Peruvians knew tobacco, but only used it as a medicine. It was used to chew, as shown here. Right, a doctor examines an infant.

Incas, was another efficient means of fighting illness. The day before the ceremony, all the sick and infirm left the town, while the healthy persons fasted. A *sanko,* a sort of corn paste to which were added a few drops of blood from a healthy

child, taken from between it eyebrows, was prepared. Later white llama's blood was used. The *sanko* was supposed to have purifying virtues. It was begun at dawn; the body was rubbed with it, and it was spread over the doorstep.

The main part of the feast took place at night. When the moon came up over the horizon, the people gathered on the main square shouted: "Ills and unhappiness begone from this country!", and four members of the royal family took up the cry. Then these four set off, each accompanied by 100 soldiers, along four roads corresponding to the cardinal points. The people of Cuzco then started to shake their clothes and made washing movements. In a kind of ritual dance, they chased away all the dangerous germs that might be on them.

The soldiers continued their run, spears in hand, chasing ills and unhappiness until they were some way out of town. Here, they stuck their spears into the ground to mark the boundary for ills of all kinds. They then bathed in a river or stream and dipped their weapons in the purifying water. They were joined by some of the people, who carried torches. The feast ended in an explosion of joy to celebrate the victory of good health.

Left and above, angles of the famous Sacsayhoaman fortress. Above, the entrance to one of the fortresses platforms.

XVI. ARTS AND SCIENCES

THE HERITAGE OF THE PAST

The year 1478 is estimated to be the year in which the Inca Empire was founded. It was an Empire more interested in social and political organization than in the development of the arts. It is not surprising then that all the works discovered from this epoch are of a utilitarian rather than decorative character.

It can be said that the Incas hardly developed the arts or sciences. They gathered the heritage of the past and chose from it what suited them best and adapted it to their mentality.

In brief, the Inca civilization was based on five great cultures. The *Chavin*, the first to be developed in the North of the Empire, the *Mochica*, which spread along the northern coast, and the *Nazca*, also from the coast, but further south (the last two were the cradles of pottery and weaving respectively). The successors to these three were the *Tihuanaco*, responsible for the monolithic blocks and statues at the south of Lake Titicaca, and the *Chimu*, whose capital, *Chan-Chan* was built on the Pacific coast.

ARCHITECTURE

If the Incas showed little interest in developing the artistic traditions they had inherited, their vision of grandeur led them to put the accent on architecture. They concentrated on building fortresses and buildings of a religious nature. These enormous constructions, some of which have resisted the passage of time, are surprising because the Incas had no knowledge of either the wheel or the vault, and used neither cement nor mortar.

On the high plateau, builders used stone, whereas they made do with adobe on the coastal plain. Some of these adobe blocks were up to three feet in size. They were covered with motifs or carved with bas-reliefs.

Before starting a building, architects made models in clay that were as accurate as possible and took the terrain into account. Only then was the project begun. To quarry the granite blocks the

Left, reconstitution of the gates to a ladies' college in Pachacamac. The curious photo on the right shows the remarkable combination of two heaps of stones at the Cuzco fortress.

Above, a gate at Tiahuanaco and bonding of stones in the military quarter of Machu Picchu.

workers drilled holes in the rock. Then they put in pieces of wood that they then wetted. The swelling wood split the stone. Then hundreds of workers carried off the blocks, attaching ropes to them and pushing as well as pulling. The stone was shaped with copper tools and by rubbing two blocks together after introducing a fine layer of wet sand between them.

The rule of thumb for architects was that all buildings had to be capable of resisting earthquakes.

This is why the base of a building was made so broad, only one floor used and virtually no windows. There were recesses at all levels to break the overall monotony.

One of the trademarks of this style of architecture was the trapezoidal shape given to doors and openings. The walls were made of irregular polygonal blocks, which fitted perfectly into one another or well aligned regular rectangles with a slightly curved outside face. There were types of extensions coming out of some stones, and it is not sure whether they were for ornamentation or supports to which roped were tied to hold down the thatched roofs.

Stone constructions represent the utility aspect of the Inca times, with their solid, uniform style. The mainly horizontal lines are stamped with majestic severity.

Among the most remarkable buildings are the fortresses, or *puracas,* of which the Sacsahuaman in Cuzco and the Ollantaytambo in the Urubamba valley appear to be the most important. As to temples, we will come back to the *Coricancha* in Cuzco, which was dedicated to the Sun.

Below, detail of the staircase at Machu Picchu and an engraving showing Inca noblemen taking part in the building of a military edifice. Right, an aspect of the Machu Picchu site.

MACHU PICCHU

Among the ruins most frequently visited today is Machu Picchu, a mysterious town situated in strange countryside, a real eagle's nest above the forests and below the peaks.

It was discovered on July 24, 1911 by Hiram Bingham, accompanied by Sergeant Carrasco. The two men, who had set out to find the capital where Manco, descendant of Atahualpa, had taken refuge, little imagined what awaited them. They got progressive glimpses of the terraces which preceded the temples, buildings of all kinds, and silent city streets.

The city of Machu Picchu was built 7,500 feet high on a ridge. It appears to be protected by two rocky peaks. It overlooks the valley where the rushing Urubamba flows. Once divided into two parts, which can still easily be distinguished today —the outskirts where peasants and soldiers lived, and the centre, home of the nobility and civil servants—its streets and staircases lead to the square where can be admired great buildings of granite. Here parades and sporting events took place.

There are 50 staircases in Machu Picchu, which have more than three thousand steps. The style of the buildings is a little different from in Cuzco. There are several two-storied buildings, which once had pointed roofs. Amongst the most remarkable buildings are the temple with its windows and the cylindrical Sun tower.

Only a few of the secrets of this unusual town have been revealed. Some of it has still not been excavated. Several doors leading to underground passages cannot be opened because of the risk of collapse and suffocation.

Machu Picchu: the site, the remains of one of its monuments, with those of a fortress and the angle of the wall of a platform.

Other remains at Machu Picchu. Right, needles with hieroglyphs from the Huayla civilization, conserved in the Lima Museum.

LANGUAGES

As the Incas spread their rule over several peoples, the dialects spoken in the Empire became more numerous. More than 600 have been counted. Three languages predominated: *Quechua, Aymara* and *Uro*. Quechua was the official language and spoken at court and taught in the only school in Cuzco. The Incas made civil servants and chiefs from subdued regions learn it. Aymara was widespread around Lake Titicaca and the high plateau. Uro, on the other hand, was only used on certain islands in the lake and disappeared progressively as Quechua and Aymara took over. These two languages survived the conquest and are still spoken today in many parts of Peru and Bolivia. They have many common phonetic

points. They both have a very extensive vocabulary and are so concise as to express whole sentences in one word. The sounds are hard and gutteral, being a succession of explosions, and baffle the European who tries to pronounce them. Many of the words have an onomatopaeic origin. For instance, to sneeze in Quechua is "atchicuni", baby "houahoua" and pain "alaou".

LITERATURE

In spite of their strange sounds, or perhaps because of them, Quechua and Aymara inspired many poets. The Incas were born romantics and expressed their melancholy or amorous feelings in short, simple and musical verses. These spoke of the lover's loneliness, the pain of not being understood, the nostalgia that the unchanging march of time brought on, or the harshness of fate.

However, the Andean people could not write. Attempts to prove that their drawings represented ideograms have remained without success. This is why their poems, tales and legends have been transmitted by oral tradition only.

The *amautas* were responsible for collecting and communicating the history of the kingdom. Emperors surrounded themselves with specialists, who were both troubadors and poets, and who passed on what they had seen and heard. When an Inca died, the *amautas* recounted the great events of his reign, giving birth to a form of ballad. These trustees and keepers of the national history were highly respected and looked after with great care.

They too passed down their knowledge to their heirs. Poems and epic poems were intoned and sung in the pentatonic scale, which was typical of Andean music.

A SUPERSTITIOUS RACE

This lack of writing prevents us from having an exact idea of the part played by astrology in Inca times. We do know that the Indians observed the sky and interpreted in their own way the phenomena that they saw there, in keeping with daily necessities.

The peasants preferred the moon to the sun, which was the official, inalterable and permanent god. The moon, with the changes that it underwent across the months, seemed more familiar to them and allowed more interpretations.

The Indians were terribly suspicious and looked constantly to the sky for signs about their future. Thus they never sowed during full moon and saw rain or drought in certain phases of the lunar cycle. If there was an orange halo around the heavenly body, the people took to praying as this meant misfortune. The appearance of a comet meant hunger, wars and epidemics. Lunar or solar eclipses were more baffling to them than any other phenomenon and put them into states of panic. For them it was the end of the world.

THE CALENDAR

Heavenly bodies have always played a practical role for farming communities. The Incas based their calendar on one sun year. They divided the sun's cycle into twelve lunar months that they grouped into periods of three months, roughly corresponding to our seasons. However, it is difficult to know how they balanced out their calendar, as the solar year exceeded the twelve lunar months by eleven days. Several theories have been put forward on this point. Nor have historians been able to agree on the length of an Inca week. Did it have five, seven or ten days. We still do not know exactly.

The Inca Pachacuti, who wanted to establish a system to fix exactly the beginning of crop sowing and other work, built 12 towers on a hill to the east of Cuzco, which were observation towers, each corresponding to a month of the year. From these towers, the people could follow the movements of the sun and moon with precision.

XVII. RELIGIOUS LIFE

GODS IN THE IMAGE OF THE INCAS

If we bear in mind the fact that the Inca Manco Capac and all those who followed him were officially sons of the Sun god *Inti,* then the close link between religion and politics is easy to understand. Veneration of the Inca was mingled with religious services. Whoever was wanting in respect for the Inca at the same time committed a crime against the Sun god. As they conquered their neighbours the Incas, while respecting local divinities, imposed on them the worship of their "ancestor", thus doubtless strengthening their political influence.

Temples to *Inti* were erected in all conquered regions. None was equal to the *Coricancha* in Cuzco. An outer wall of great beauty surrounded very simple buildings built on the model of private houses and with thatched roofs, which was the only type of roof then used, both for palaces and huts. The main decoration was a frieze which ran along the whole length of the wall as well as the walls fo the sanctuaries, and which was made of gold plating applied directly to the masonry. Only the nobility could enter these places, and then they had to be barefoot. There was also a little garden where the Inca dug symbolically at sowing time and where he also plated golden ears of corn, three times a year.

One of the five buildings which acted as the actual temple, held the mummies of dead emperors and empresses. They were brought out of the temple and carried around on stretchers at important feasts.

Viracocha, Creator and Supreme Being, stood above the Sun. His worship became important during Pachacuti's reign and supplanted somewhat that of *Inti.* There might be a political explanation in this phenomenon or perhaps a religious one. One can see a legitimate desire—common to all Indians—to explain the genesis of the world. Viracocha appeared to Pachacuti in a dream and became his special protector. The Inca built a temple in his honour with a statue in gold. Viracocha, besides being Creator, was also considered as Civilizer and Changer of Things. The Inca followed in his footsteps.

Left, the entrance of a great temple dedicated to the Moon, in Tiahuanaco. Right the statue of an Inca divinity (conserved in La Paz).

Left, vase in the shape of a temple with a priest (Chicago Museum). Above, reconstitution of the "Del Cerro Blanco" temple in Lima.

Viracocha gave men "precepts that they had to respect under pain of being overwhelmed by him", a chronicler relates. In the god's footsteps, Pachacuti lost no time in promulgating laws. It is interesting to note that the god was represented on the frescoes in the Sun temple by an enormous egg, the symbol of creation.

Viracocha was essentially good. The Indians turned to him when they needed reassurance. In their prayers, they asked him for peace and safety. "Preserve those you have made" they said, "and hold us by the hand". Viracocha, the master of the universe, to whom "sun, moon, day, night, summer and winter" were subject, as the Inca prayer said, was present everywhere and sought everywhere, always ready to listen to his subjects, and was not unlike the Christian god.

Another god was *Inti Illapa,* lord of thunder and lightening, rain and hail. Temples were built to him and he was implored from the summits of mountains when drought threatened the crops.

As to the Moon, which often appears in Poma de Ayala's drawings beside the Sun, it was revered as sister and wife of the latter. It was mainly worshipped on the coast, as it favoured night fishing, as well as nocturnal picking of magic herbs.

HUACAS, SACRED OBJECTS

If the gods which we have spoken of were mainly objects of devotion in Cuzco and the towns, in the country, family divinities such as *cenopas* and *huacas* were more common. The former, which looked after the prosperity of the household, were generally statuettes of wood or metal, miniature reproductions of man and woman, with their woollen clothing, while the latter could either be natural monuments suchas hills, rocks, caves, lakes (Lake Titicaca, for example) or buildings of all kinds.

It was generally the Incas themselves who decided on the sacred aspect of a particular huaca by resting, bathing or taking an important decision in the place. The place could also present a

129

Various remains of Tiahuanaco, mainly monoliths which were used as markers for the ground of a great temple and divinity.

Above, women weaving. Right, a priest (this can be guessed from his mitre).

supernatural aspect, such as a grotto where it was believed hail formed or earthquakes were thought to start.

Huacas were most often little sacred boulders. Many legends claim that they were men turned into stone. The meaning of the word *huaca* is obscure. It is thought that it simply meant any object in which a spirit was embodied. Many huacas were guardian divinities, directly attached to an *ayllu*. In this way they became the incarnation of an ancestor of the curaca, coming to his aid to help him exercice his power. Once again religion became intertwined with politics.

Besides cloth, the main offering made to huacas was chicha. The Spanish missionaries were shocked to see worship of such a kind and soon put a stop to these pagan activities. However, ethnologists today are finding similar practices again, proving that four centuries of Christianity have not totally obliterated the influence of the huacas.

PRIESTS AND "SUN VIRGINS"

Priests were numerous and often feared. They were also organized in an hierarchy at the head of which was *Vilca-oma*, the high priest, chosen by the Inca at his accession from among his brothers and uncles. He officiated at the *Coricancha*, primarily assisted by ten other priests of importance. There was a total of 4,000 religious and lay personnel in the temple.

While the members of the lower clergy received their plot of earth to cultivate like the peasants, the high priests were supported by the state and bound to chastity and temperance. The curacas' families provided the leading priests who were assigned to provincial cities, Sun temples and the most important huacas. Each huaca was in fact looked after by a man of the church.

The Vilca-oma's residence was situated near Cuzco, so that he could go to the city every day, while having the possibility to observe and meditate on the sky every evening. His clothes were simple, except for feast days, when he was dressed in white and crowned, it is thought, with a golden tiara. He nominated the members of the high clergy—practically all members of the nobility—who in turn chose the lower clergy. He also designated the inspectors who roamed the Empire to control sanctuaries and choose the girls who, with the daughters of the nobility, would become the "Sun Virgins".

It was Garcilaso de la Vega who first gave them this name. Their Quechua name was in fact *aclla-cuna,* which simply meant "chosen woman". Taken from among the most beautiful and noble females, the Sun Virgins lived as recluses from the age of eight, or at least before they were twelve, at which time a strict selection was made after careful preparation. The best were admitted as novices and three years later, following an examination, were confirmed as aclla-cuna, the others becoming their servants. Dressed in white, and chaste under threat of terrible punishments (even the village of a girl unfortunate enough not to obey could be razed to the ground in reprisal, and the girl tortured to death), the Sun Virgins carried out various tasks. They prepared the chicha which was used in abundance both as an offering and a drink at ceremonies, weaved, spun and brocaded the finest wools to make the awnings for the temples or the Inca's and the royal family's clothing. They were also entrusted with making *llautu* and *mascapaicha*

133

which made up the royal head-dress. They watched over the sacred flame which was lit at the feast of *Inti Raymi.*

There were no less than 1,500 Sun Virgins cloistered in Cuzco. They were of royal blood, daughters of curacas and some were of peasant stock from convents in the provincial capitals. None of them had the right to be in contact with their families. It was in these cloisters that the Inca chose his wives. Other virgins were offered, as we have seen in a previous chapter, to civil servants of merit and others were... sacrificed. More of this later.

CONFESSIONS AND SACRIFICES

The Inca religion bore a close similarity to Catholicism (the Spanish missionaries saw it as an odious parody), and had as much political as religious meaning. All kinds of mishap, such as the illness of a leading personality, unfavourable climatic conditions, etc, were pretext for all kinds of inquiries which aimed at finding human causes for phenomena which were anything but that and also provided the opportunity to force every subject to a real examination of his conscience. There was sure to be a malcontent somewhere who had complained about the emperor, had disobeyed a superior or attempted some act of witchcraft. If he confessed and payed for his crime, then order would return.

The whole exercise then was intended to discover offences against social order or nature, and not "sins" against the established morality. It is claimed, however, that this practice helped Catholicism gain its dominance.

Chroniclers tell how penitent and confessor finally

"spat" out the sin onto a tuft of grass or into a little bag, which was then thrown into water as a sign of purification. Sometimes the guilty man washed his misdeeds in a stream or river.

In addition the gods demanded human and animal sacrifices. This was an astonishing practice for a people so prudent and so inclined to economy. However, there is no doubt that it was a fact, at least at the time of the first Incas. Young people in good health were killed, and even infants in arms, which were carefully fed before being offered. These sacrifices were obviously performed only in exceptional circumstances. They were the last resort, not only in a situation of danger, but, para-doxically, following a natural catastrophe like an earthquake. It seems that certain great events were even accompanied by human sacrifices.

These sacrifices were, however, gradually replaced by llama sacrifices, a brown animal for Viracocha, a white one for the Sun, and a mottled one for Thunder. Under the influence of Pachacuti, who was shocked by so much waste, the llamas and guinea pigs—offered by the poor—were substituted by statuettes that represented them. Gold, silver and wood figurines, in the image of man and woman, were also burned or buried in place of real people. Wisdom and a spirit of economy thus won the day over religious fanaticism.

Pacha Camac: the remains of the temple and the reconstitution of the womens' houses.

Huaca-Kenko: On the left, the passage from the sacred place to the sacrifical hemicycle (shown in the photo opposite). Above, the stairway of a corridor. Below, an instrument in the shape of a star used to fracture the skulls of those being sacrificed.

unricuna

pacharama maypimca

las yñs

THE FESTIVAL OF THE SUN

Viracocha and Inti were complementary gods. The first represented earth, water and mountain, the second sky, fire and forest. The most glittering of all festivals was dedicated to the latter—the Sun festival or *Intiraymi*. It was celebrated at the winter solstice in the southern hemisphere, which is in June. Curacas and civil servants came from all regions to the capital to take part, accompanied by lamas and presents. The most gorgeous clothes were worn and visitors could therefore easily see who was taking part among the grey mass of the inhabitants of Cuzco. The richest curacas came on palanquins. They could be distinguished by their different headgear.

On the morning of the raymi, after three days of fasting and sexual abstinence, the members of the imperial ayllus gathered on the main square of Cuzco, while the curacas met on a neighbouring square. The Inca joined them before the dawn. They all removed their shoes and waited in silence for sunrise. When the first rays appeared, only the Inca remained standing, holding a cup in each hand, which he invited the god to drink from. The others, who were squatting down, blew noisy kisses to the rays which touched them and stretched their arms as a sign of devotion.

The monarch then poured the cup into a narrow channel which carried chicha, prepared by the Sun Virgins, to the nearby temple then drank from the cup in his left hand before passing it to his neighbours. Then the nobles entered the Sun temple to offer cups and gifts to the god. The curacas were not allowed into the sanctuary, but their presents were accepted by the priests at the entrance.

The sacrifices began with the killing of a black llama, which was considered as the animal in its purest shape—the white llama had a speckled snout. The soothsayer examined the entrails, and if the portents were not favourable, another couple of llamas were slaughtered to try and find more reassuring signs. The god was then asked to light a fire using a concave mirror and pieces of dry cotton. This sacred flame was then placed in the sanctuary and guarded by "chosen women" until the next year.

Other animals were also sacrificed. Their meat was cooked on the square and offered to those present.

However, it sometimes happened that the god

did not deign to show himself. This was obviously seen as the most terrible portent and the fire was lit by rubbing pieces of wood together.

Once the religious part of the ceremony was over, the Inca invited his children to drink, starting with the most worthy. For this he held identical cups in his hands as before. Then, in response to a principal of reciprocity that was dear to the Incas, the children offered the grown-ups drinks. The Inca only wet his lips, otherwise he would have been dead drunk with so much hard liquor. Each cup that he touched was considered as sacred and no one dared to use them. They belonged to the family treasure. The festivities lasted for nine days, passed in singing and dancing; the chicha flowed like water.

DEATHS AND BURIALS

The Peruvian Indians were firm believers in a life after death. Was it a reincarnation or life in the unknown? Ideas varied according to places,

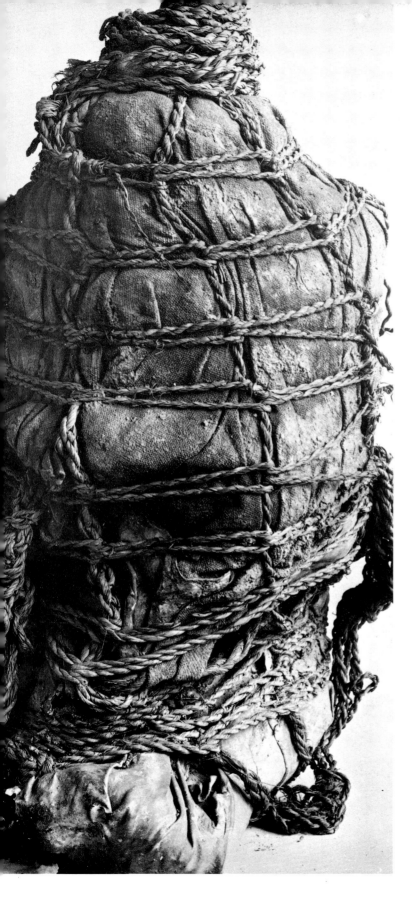

customs and traditions. In the Jauja region, for example, the dead were wrapped in a llama skin and sewn up, probably in the belief that the dead person would return in the shape of an animal. Tombs were often filled with objects that were intended to accompany the dead person in a future life. Important people were buried with containers filled with huge supplies of food, clean and pressed clothes, instruments and weapons which they had used, and part of their wealth. The chronicler Cobo tells how gold and silver were put into their mouths, hands and on their breasts and elsewhere. The poor were accompanied only by their tools, a few ears of corn and a little chicha.

The Incas and nobles were mummified. This guaranteed their survival; the techniques were rudimentary but efficient. The body was treated with certain products such as menthol, wrapped in cotton and put into bags, with the limbs free to move. The head was sometimes put inside this envelope and therefore replaced on the outside with a wooden effigy. The mummies, or *malqui*, generally had a golden mask. In a sitting position, with the legs folded into the body, the hands on the chest, they almost gave the impression of being alive when they were carried through the town.

Death was accepted with serenity, and as a natural consequence of life. Pachacuti even composed a poem at the end of his days.

"I was born like a lily in the garden
And it is thus I grew
Time has passed and I have grown old
On the eve of departing I wither
and I die"

The fact that the Indians placed the corpse in a foetal position indicated that they were completing the cycle of life.

The newly-deceased Inca was immediately followed to the tomb by those of his wives who wanted to and by the number of servants that he would need in the next world.

The death ceremonies—dressing of the body and preparation for burial—took place in darkness and were followed by weeping and sad, slow dances, which varied in length, so the chroniclers say, according to the rank and importance of the deceased. All this was accompanied by a meal taken in common, where drink predominated.

On these pages, two symbols of the Inca civilization: weaving designs and a excavation at Machu Picchu, with a stone that still has to be interpreted.

OMENS

Priests who did not serve in the temples or huacas were divided into many categories. Their jobs were mainly as sorcerers or soothsayers, catering for a people whose superstition was famous.

Omens resulted in sacrifices, mainly of llamas, and entrails and heart were examined. A chronicler relates how before a battle faltering llamas—they had been starved—were sacrificed. The almost lifeless hearts of these animals in the open chest represented the weak hearts of the soldiers' enemies. Sometimes birds were burned and the spirit of the deceased was called up by blowing on the flames in the hearth.

Sculptures of the time show soothsayers blowing into lungs to find the traces of the blood vessels. Spiders, their webs and their way of walking were observed, as well as snakes, the flight of certain birds, corn seeds, rainbows and heavenly bodies. Dreams were of great importance and love potions were prepared.

A WORLD APART

The trial and execution of the Inca Atahualpa by Pizarro was the sign for the end of the Empire. So disappeared a world, not without its contradictions, but whose organization was closely adapted to the native mentality of its inhabitants and which was remarkably unified from the political, economic and religious points of view. It was a society based on the principles of safety and dignity, even for those who lived in the less favoured regions and on that of reciprocity: *give and it shall be returned to you.*

Within its framework, the Indians applied the Quechua precepts, one of which is worth quoting here to show their greatness: *Nucanquis purinanchis nanun puscananchis:* the strong man who cries with the weak man will live.

143